THE INTIMACY JUNGLE

To Mitchell,
Wishing you the best!
Terry Parsons

THE INTIMACY JUNGLE

HOW YOU CAN SURVIVE AND THRIVE IN A LASTING MARRIAGE

by

Terry Parsons, Ph.D., D.Min.

BROWN BOOKS
PUBLISHING GROUP

Second Printing 2004
Third Printing 2017

ISBN 978-0-9702634-0-7

Published by:
Brown Books, Dallas

www.brownbooks.com

This book is dedicated to my wife, Kathleen, with whom I have survived and thrived in our own intimacy jungle, and to my parents, Anderson and Ruby Parsons, who demonstrated what it really takes to have a lifetime marriage.

Dr. Terry Parsons has keen insight and a remarkable way of sharing it. His wise counsel is laced with humor and personal experience for people who trying to share the joys of life together. These are words to live "by" and words to live "with." *The Intimacy Jungle* will be my close companion from the tropics to frozen tundra, wherever I may roam.

Jeff Eliasoph
Television News Anchor

CONTENTS

ACKNOWLEDGMENTS

I always read the acknowledgments in a book because I know many people have helped to develop a writer's dream into a published reality. I am humbly and gratefully aware of this collaborative effort.

I thank my wife, Kathleen, for being my constant and loving companion since we met in a cafeteria at Southern Methodist University in February 1971. With her, I have learned in a very poignant and personal way what it means to find the right mate, develop an intimate relationship, and survive and thrive in a lifetime marriage. I am grateful for her patience during my years of schooling, researching, and writing.

I thank our children, Laura and Adam, for being the special people they are and for adding so much learning, growth, love, challenge, and joy to our lives. I really appreciate their support and encouragement regarding this project—"Dad, when is your book going to be published?"

I thank John Gladfelter, Ph.D., my psychology mentor, for his years of wise counsel and steady influence. I thank Bernard I. Murstein, Ph.D., for his pioneering research about mate selection, and for his valuable comments regarding my research.

I am greatly indebted to the 108 couples who gave their time and shared valuable, intimate information about their relationships for this study. I thank the scores of couples who participated in the preliminary studies for contributing an abundance of data crucial for the final research project.

I thank the thousands of couples I have worked with in therapy sessions and in COMMIT and THRIVE seminars. I respect their courage and willingness to open up and share who they are; to confront, struggle with, and work through their issues; to laugh, cry, and rejoice as they change and grow in their lives as individuals and in their relationships. I sometimes feel like Moses—that I need to take off my shoes because these are "holy ground" experiences.

I thank Tom Payton, Ed.D., for being my good friend and colleague. I thank my many friends for their love and care. I thank the churches and various organizations that have afforded me the opportunity to share the good news of COMMIT and THRIVE.

I thank Larry Holden, writer and senior editor for *Country Weekly* magazine, for reading and re-reading my manuscript and helping me to write less like a scholar and more like a journalist. His writing and editing skills and his encouragement to keep re-writing helped this book to communicate what I really wanted to express.

I thank my publisher, Milli Brown, and her staff for believing in me and this book. I appreciate their expertise in helping my dream become a reality.

I thank God.

INTRODUCTION

It's a jungle out there. A jungle more deadly than any alligator-infested swamp. A jungle more treacherous than any rainforest crawling with 30-foot-long pythons. It's the intimacy jungle—where your happiness and fulfillment for a lifetime are at stake.

Do you want a thriving, lifetime marriage? If you do, this book is for you. It will identify the factors that are absolutely essential to a lasting relationship. These factors are illustrated with intriguing real-life examples and carefully designed exercises to help you thrive in your unique relationship.

You may be dating, engaged, married, single, separated, or divorced. You may be lonely, scared, confused, hurt, hopeful, or happy. Whatever your status or feelings, like most of us, you want a healthy and solid intimate relationship. For years, my personal, professional, and scholarly goal has been to help individuals and couples regarding mate selection, relationship development, and marriage. This powerful, positive, passionate, and sometimes humorous book will help you make your relationship a thriving and incredible journey.

What makes *The Intimacy Jungle* so special?

Although a number of books have been written about mate selection and marriage, this book is unique because it is based on scientific research. Most books about these subjects are based on informal, intuitive kinds of inquiry. There is nothing wrong with these approaches; they have provided much useful information. However, using the best available research methods for a subject as important as a successful, lifetime marriage is just as important as using the best available research methods to understand the fundamentals of transportation systems and the environment. Vehicles, clean water, and people wanting good marriages are very different issues. But each is uniquely important for surviving and thriving in the jungle.

Most social science research about mate selection has focused on sociocultural variables and generalized theoretical models. Also, unmarried college students have traditionally been the subjects selected for studies about mate selection. While the results of these studies have yielded useful information, they have not addressed the void of information in the literature about the complex process of mate selection and relationship development *from the perspective of married couples.*

Even studies using married persons usually have a much higher participation by females than males, resulting in incomplete data. My research was based on 108 couples, making the participation by females and males equal. These couples had been married only once, and had been married 2 months to 56 years.

My study involved identifying 36 items that were most important to married couples. These qualities of attraction, relationship development, and compatibility are discussed throughout the book.

The items under *attraction* are:

**physical attractiveness*
**socio-economic background*
**level of education*
**race or ethnic origin*
**sexual attractiveness*
**personality characteristics*
**age*
**intelligence*

family background
religious background
intense romantic feelings
physical attraction

The items under *relationship development* are:

comparing our family backgrounds
comparing interests and hobbies
comparing handling of financial matters
friends' approval of our marrying
comparing values regarding commitment and fidelity
discussing our sexual expectations and interests
comparing values and religious beliefs
expressing thoughts and feelings to each other
parents' approval of our marrying
learning to resolve problems and conflicts
comparing social and political values
discussing career goals

The items under *compatibility* are:

how we practice our religious beliefs and/or values
agreeing with each other about spending and saving money
expressing appreciation and affection to each other
compatibility regarding interests and hobbies
relationship with each other's families
agreement regarding time spent with friends or in activities
companionship
spouse's work/career
having a satisfying and fulfilling sex life
how we deal with our child/children
receiving emotional support from my spouse
how we balance our roles and responsibilities

I was interested to see how these items might change in

importance from the couples' first meeting, during their courtship, when they married, and at the present time in their marriage. I was also interested in comparing, decade by decade, the possible difference of these items for couples who married from the 1940s to the 1990s.

In addition to a scientific, scholarly research model, this book offers powerful illustrations based on my experiences with thousands of couples over the past 25 years as a counselor and minister. I have gained intriguing insight from couples in my research, in my counseling sessions, and in seminars and retreats. The combination of scholarly research involving married couples and thousands of hours of counseling sessions with couples both married and unmarried sets this book apart from other efforts. *The Intimacy Jungle* reveals what is really important in mate selection, relationship development, and marriage.

I am currently conducting seminars based on material in this book. COMMIT is a series for dating and engaged couples. THRIVE is a series for married couples. Also, my own experiences concerning these items from more than 25 years of marriage to my beautiful and loving wife, Kathleen, contribute to my understanding of a lasting relationship.

If we marry, *whom* we marry is for most of us one of the most lasting relationship decisions we ever make. Whether we stay married for a lifetime or for a short while, this decision profoundly affects our entire lives. Although most people do marry, many marriages either end in painful divorce or sink into the quicksand of day-to-day unhappiness.

Most people truly desire a fulfilling, lifetime marriage. What can we do to help ensure this most important intimate relationship journey? You have already had your share of personal and relationship experiences. Some of you have read self-help books. Still others have had some form of personal, relationship, or family therapy.

I often say I do not do "cookie-cutter" therapy because I do not counsel cookie-cutter people. No theoretical model will work for all of us. We are each unique and our relationships are unique.

I have written this book to provide you with the best available information and I have included exercises at the end of each chapter. These exercises are specifically designed so that you can explore your own personal and relationship issues. They will significantly benefit you, whether you are dating, engaged, married, single, separated, or divorced.

The Intimacy Jungle is a guide for thriving in your own process of mate selection, relationship development, and marriage. I encourage you to read it with *pen in hand*, so that you can underline and take notes, making this a personally useful companion for your most amazing relationship journey. I hope this book becomes a cherished friend that travels with you often. I wish you the best as you not only *survive* but *thrive* in the intimacy jungle!

PART ONE:
THE JUNGLES WE COME FROM

Chapter 1
The Jungles of Mate Selection

I Want Someone I Can Survive With in This Jungle

He was a hairy, strong-jawed young man hunting for food. He had roamed farther than ever before, coming to the edge of the jungle he'd known since birth. Suddenly, he stood motionless in the thick undergrowth. He peered across a clearing at the unfamiliar jungle 100 yards away. He cocked his head, a curious expression upon his youthful face.

Then his eyes fixed on something moving near the edge of the strange new jungle. A ferocious tiger? Another kind of predator?

As the creature stood up, he could see it was somewhat like himself, except more curvaceous, like his mother. The she-creature was picking berries.

His eyes widened with excitement as she stood and looked in his direction. They stared at each other for several minutes. His heart raced. He had no sisters and had never seen a young female like this in his small village.

Then he made a bold decision. He stepped from his familiar jungle into the clearing toward the attractive female. At first, she started to turn away. Then she turned back and started walking cautiously in his direction. He was curious, interested, excited—and scared.

"What will I do when I get close to her?" he wondered.

As she approached, his fears were replaced by desire. He exhaled a pleased "*Umm!*" She uttered a soft "*Ugh.*"

Finally, they stood face to face. They looked into each other's expressive eyes. He smiled. She smiled. He hesitated, then held out his hand. She took it. They ate berries while they sat on a grassy mound in the clearing between their respective jungles. Then he gently picked her up and carried her into his jungle.

When the young male, Ugh, and the young female, Umm met, *thriving* was not a goal. *Surviving* was the name of the game.

In primitive cultures, physical survival was the focus of all aspects of life, from daily food gathering to mate selection. A mate who was big, strong, and hairy was important to both females and males. Subtle qualities, such as sensitivity and sleek physiques, were not the order of the day when protecting life and limb were at stake. Ugh's guttural marriage proposal to Umm might be translated: "I want you to be with me because together we may be able to survive the dangers of this jungle."

Centuries later, in most cultures on the "flat" earth, parents dictated or directed their children's choice of a mate. These patriarchal societies not only treated women like property, they treated children the same way; indeed, mate selection was a matter of a union contracted by heads of families when the children to wed were quite young. A marriage contract in those days might have been communicated in this way, between the fathers of, say, Nadab and Rivka: "Our lineage is a fine one. Nadab is heir to that and one day he will have all of my wealth and power as well. If you will offer 20 camels, 20 cows, 20 sheep, and your daughter, we will have a deal and a wedding. Then, when Nadab and Rivka are older, you and I will have many grandsons to hold this land and more." Granddaughters weren't considered significant in those days, though they were of course necessary to keep the species going.

Also, being big and physically strong wasn't particularly important to the dealing dads or to the marriage brokers hired by families to decide who married whom; some slightly subtler considerations had become more significant. If your family did not have much wealth or power to offer, or if you were number 13 in birth order, you might never marry. Such was fate in those times.

Prearranged marriages served economic and political purposes for families in societies in which individual identity was secondary to prescribed roles in life. The shift from mate selection being dominated by parents to being the result of romantic love was the product of evolutionary historical and social change. The idea of romantic love, which would radically affect the institutions of family and marriage in much of the Western world, started in the early Middle Ages.

At first, however, romantic love did not lead to marriage; indeed, it was viewed as being utterly distinct from and opposed to marriage, which was still very much a matter of social and family alliances rather than of individual choice. For that reason, Charles might lament to Suzette, "I love you with all my heart, but our parents have promised us to others."

From the 14th to the 18th century, romantic love became more associated with marriage, though it still was far from being causative to it. Romance, carefully sanitized and supervised, became a kind of grace note for the still essentially pragmatic business of a sound marriage.The result was that, following a formal betrothal, the man romanced the woman to win the bride-to-be's affection during their courtship.

A courtship scene during this time might find William bringing freshly-picked flowers to Anne, who would walk and converse with him. William might nervously say to his arranged fiancée: "I find you to be more beautiful than these flowers and I hope you will come to find me worthy of your affection." William may have truly believed what he was saying and Anne may have too. At least, they both were probably hoping that they would develop a loving relationship.

In the 19th century, the cart and horse began to switch places. Marriage no longer had to come *before* love. People were free to choose their own mates. Finally, a couple's romance and courtship could precede their engagement rather than *following* a betrothal arranged by their parents. Instead of parents choosing mates for their children, the children became their own authorities in making these choices. *This is one of the greatest shifts in the history of relationships*.

In a 1950's scene, as Debbie's father sat in his chair with a serious expression on his face, 22-year-old Johnny gulped and explained, "I love Debbie very much. I have a good job. And I want to ask you for Debbie's hand in marriage." If Debbie's dad did not consent, Johnny and Debbie could still elope—because they were their own authorities about getting married.

That scene, once common in the '50s, changed considerably during the last half of the 20th century. The length of courtship increased, as numerous couples lived together without getting married. Or lived together *before* they married. Also, age at the time of marriage was generally greater in the '60s, '70s, '80s, and '90s than in previous decades. And there was a significant increase in the number of divorces and remarriages.

Beyond the millennium and into the 21st century, more "couple-directed" marital scenes will be common. Maria and Dion are likely to call their parents in New York from her apartment in Los Angeles and leave a voice mail message proclaiming: "Hey, we just wanted to let you guys know we're getting married July 12th, and we'd love for you to fly out and celebrate this great time with us!"

Throughout history, the "jungles" have changed. Today, instead of thick undergrowth with saber-tooth tigers as real dangers, we have steel and glass skyscrapers, with high divorce rates being among the pitfalls. But every culture has developed rituals to address mate selection practices. There was Ugh and Umm's survival-of-the-fittest coupling. Nadab and Rivka's participation in their dads' social-financial arrangement. Charles and Suzette's hearts for each other, but marriages to their parents' choices. William's attempt to win the affection of Anne, who was selected for him. Johnny asking Deb's dad for her hand in marriage. And now, Maria and Dion telling their parents they are getting married.

Today, couples want to do more than simply *survive*. They want to *thrive* in this life-changing, life-affirming relationship journey.

Do Parents Still Influence Mate Selection?

Each of you can answer this question based on your experience with your own parents. This is a crucial issue to address because our parents' influence on each of us is significant. Their influence affects choice of a mate and marriage. From Ugh and Umm's parents to Maria and Dion's parents, mothers and fathers want their children's relationships with their mates to be rewarding ones.

Although Western parents may no longer arrange marriages, most of us are aware that parental influence is present in our selecting—or not selecting—a mate. As therapists, my colleagues and I may sometimes comment, "Sounds like you married your mother." Or, "Sounds like you married your father."

Psychoanalytic statements such as these must make Freud smile knowingly, while making patients wince uncomfortably. The longer I've studied the issue of parental influence on mate selection, the more apparent it becomes to me that unconscious influences are extremely difficult to research.

As difficult as parental influence is to research, we can recall closely observing our parents when we were children. Basically, boys learn what it means to be male, a man, and a husband, from their fathers. Girls primarily learn what it means to be female, a woman, and a wife, from their mothers. Both observe what marriage is from the model their parents exhibit. When children play house or dress up, they may reproduce long sequences of behavior similar to what they have observed their parents doing.

We carry these models of behavior into adulthood. More often than not, when people comment that we are acting just like our fathers or mothers, it is not a compliment. Sometimes we catch ourselves and lament that the behavior we hated in a parent—*things we swore we would never do*—we do. Our childhood observation of powerful models of nurture or abuse affects us, even if we'd rather it didn't.

While observation is responsible for a large portion of social learning, certain complex behavior patterns may be developed through our emotional relationships with parents. One example is the identification process, in which the child incorporates certain values, attitudes, and behaviors of the parent. You are probably aware of some of your values, attitudes, and behaviors which are similar to those of your parents.

Your relationship with the parent of the opposite sex may serve as a rehearsal for your relationship with other people of the opposite sex. Those parent experiences may affect how acceptable and lovable you see yourself as being. Adolescent girls and boys, or adult women and men, may believe they are acceptable and lovable because their opposite-sex parents helped them to experience these feelings.

Another aspect of the quality of the emotional relationship a child has with parents, which may affect later relationship development, concerns the relationship between one's father and mother. The emotional support the child observes the father giving the mother, for example, contributes significantly to the beliefs and expectations the child develops concerning the nature of intimate relationships.

These beliefs and expectations about husband-wife relationships are further affected by the quality of the emotional relationship the child has with the father and mother. For example, the relationship the child has with the same-sex parent may affect the child's own role beliefs and expectations as a spouse. And the emotional relationship the child observes between parents will likely affect the child's role expectations of another person in an intimate relationship.

Steve and Sally

A couple, Steve and Sally, dealt with these issues of parental influence. Steve was a 25-year-old college graduate who worked in the computer industry. Sally was a 22-year-old daycare worker who had completed a two-year college program in her field. Both were physically attractive. Steve was clean-cut, muscular, and quite *independent*. Sally was pretty, soft-spoken, and quite *dependent*.

They had met at a party 14 months before they scheduled a session with me. They had broken up once for a couple of weeks after dating six months. Sally's boss had suggested she and Steve might benefit from counseling. They were considering marriage, but had recurring fights. Sally wanted Steve to spend more time with her and to be less critical of her. Steve felt that Sally was trying to control him.

Steve's dad was a career military man. He was often away from home traveling. When he was home, he was emotionally abusive to his wife, though he praised his son for being the "man of the house" while he was away.

Steve vividly remembered his father's typical homecomings when he was on leave from his sea duty. Steve was always excited to see his dad, who would bring him special gifts and tell him about the interesting places he'd visited. They would spend a lot of time together playing baseball, watching sports on television, going fishing.

But Steve's parents had difficulty adjusting to being together after their times apart. Steve painfully recalled his dad yelling at his mom because she did not keep up their house and yard to his standards. And she was gaining weight. Later, his dad would talk to Steve and apologize to him that he had to hear the yelling. Then he would brag on him for being "such a good young man."

Steve identified with his father's strong model and developed a similar attitude toward women. As a result, Steve did not spend much time with Sally and was, on occasion, emotionally abusive to her.

How, or why, would Sally put up with someone who behaved the way Steve did?

Sally's father was physically abusive to her mother. Sally qualified and minimized the abuse by saying her dad only pushed and slapped her mother. She said he never hit her with a fist or kicked her. In addition, her mother told Sally she loved her husband so much she put up with the abuse.

This was the marriage model Sally grew up with. Sally was close to and identified with her mother, so she justified Steve's behavior to herself with the thought that at least Steve did not physically abuse her.

Both Steve and Sally were living out male and female roles and relationships they had learned by observing their parents. These roles and patterns of behavior were familiar to them. But the appeal of familiarity notwithstanding, they were aware they wanted to have a better relationship than their parents.

When Steve and Sally came to therapy, I asked both of them what they wanted to change about themselves that would be beneficial for them as individuals and for their relationship. Sally said she wanted Steve to spend more time with her and to not be verbally abusive. Steve said he wanted Sally to not nag him so much when he wanted to spend time with his buddies.

These are very typical responses. Usually, we want others to change. *If "they" would change, life would be a lot better.*

I asked Sally if she thought she could change Steve. She smiled sheepishly and said, "I've tried, but he's too stubborn for anyone to change him." She then said that she wanted to become more secure within herself and less dependent upon Steve.

Steve said that he wanted to be more aware of how he was being verbally abusive to Sally. And he wanted to stop putting her down.

Sally and Steve's comments gave us issues to work on. The good news is that both Sally and Steve were willing to look at themselves and the ways they each wanted to change that would benefit them as individuals and benefit their relationship.

As a therapist, I don't think it is expedient to dwell on the past. On the other hand, I believe it is important for us to be aware of our past so that we can deal with it effectively, instead of allowing our past to control our present. Also, I don't think fixating on blaming parents is usually beneficial. Still, it is important for us to openly confront our parent issues. That way, we examine and understand those issues so that they do not sabotage our present lives and relationships.

Both Steve and Sally were able to recall experiences of undesirable behavior exhibited by, and between, their parents. Both remembered feeling scared when they overheard their parents fighting. When we observe or overhear such behaviors of our parents, we may feel scared, insecure, or angry. Also, we draw conclusions and/or make decisions about men and women, husbands and wives, marriage and ourselves, in light of these experiences.

Steve had concluded that women nag, so he determined the best way to deal with that irritating behavior was to stay out of earshot. That's what his dad did. Steve had also decided, as a child, that it was acceptable for a man to yell at a woman "to keep her in line." These were childhood decisions that Steve re-enacted in his relationship with Sally.

Sally recalled deciding as a child that she would not allow a man to physically abuse her. She had also decided that she wanted attention from her father, and, like her mother, she would nag to get it.

Parental influence is both genetic and relational. We inherit certain physical, mental, and emotional traits from our parents. And we develop various attitudes, beliefs, and behaviors from our parents. Even so, I do not believe our lives are determined by our parents.

We are unique individuals. I continue to be amazed how children from the same gene pool and the same environment can be so different. We *can* grow, learn, and change. We *can* make our own decisions. We *do not* have to live out unhealthy decisions we made as children to survive in the families in which we were reared.

I asked Sally and Steve what they wanted to change about themselves and their relationship. Sally concluded that she wanted to be stronger, to be more assertive, and to take charge of her own life. Also, she did not want to nag Steve.

Next, I asked Sally to imagine her dad sitting in a chair in my office. Then she emotionally confronted her "dad."

Sally began her "dialogue" with her "dad" by softly saying, "Dad, there are some feelings I've held inside for a long time. But I've been afraid to tell you how angry I've been. These are feelings I've had since I was a child."

The emotional "dialogue" concluded when Sally strongly and resolutely exclaimed, "I *will not* allow you, Steve, or anyone else to physically or emotionally abuse me! *I* am in charge of my life!"

Sally really did feel stronger. She took some deep breaths. She—not her dad or Steve—was in charge of her breathing. She was in charge of her thoughts. She was in charge of her emotions. *She was in charge of her life!* She was also aware that God was as close to her as the breath she breathed. With God's help, she was even stronger!

Sally committed to take "breathing breaks." Several times each day she would take deep breaths to re-enforce her decision, feelings, and strength.

Sally then addressed her "mom" using the "empty chair" exercise.

"Mom, I know you love me very much. And I love you so much. You have been very good to me. But there are a couple of things about you that really bother me. You never stood up to Dad. You allowed him to physically abuse you and to humiliate you. Also, you nagged him all the time."

After a few emotionally moving "exchanges" with her "mom," Sally took several empowering breaths. Then she stated in a clear, emphatic voice, "I will *not* be a nagging victim. *I will not be a nagging victim.* I will not be a nagging victim!"

Steve was impressed with Sally's new strength. He then confronted his "dad" and "mother" using the same exercise.

"Dad," he began quietly, "I really enjoyed the good times we had with each other. I know you loved me. But now I realize how badly you treated Mom. With me standing in the same room with you, you would yell at her. You would put her down."

With his volume increasing, Steve continued, "You were really cruel to her. You treated her like dirt. And I began to put her down too. Like you, I grew to treat her with no respect. Now, Dad, I've been treating Sally the same way."

After emotionally expressing his feelings, Steve came to some life-changing conclusions. He decided he, too, was in charge of his thoughts, his emotions, and his life. "I *will not* treat Sally the way you treated Mom. And, Dad, it feels really good to say that."

Then Steve addressed his "mom" in the other chair. "Mom, I'm really sorry for the cruel ways I have treated you. I'm going to visit you in person and apologize for being so disrespectful to you. You were always there for me. I love you. I want you to know from this moment on exactly how I'm going to view you, Sally and other women—with equal value and worth. I am *determined* to treat women with respect."

Steve said he would also take some "breathing breaks" every day. During these times, he decided to include visualizing treating his mother and Sally with respect, honor, and love.

Both Sally and Steve committed to pray for God's help each day to become the people they decided to be. Sally exclaimed, "It's like being a whole new person!"

In the next session with Sally and Steve, we explored specific ways they wanted to improve their lives and relationship.

Sally followed through with her plans by attending painting classes and playing tennis with another woman from work. She decided that if Steve became emotionally abusive, she would tell him to stop, rather than ducking her head and feeling hurt. If Steve continued the abuse, she knew she now had the inner strength to leave him.

Steve kept his commitment to treat Sally respectfully. He did not put her down or criticize her. He and Sally scheduled specific times they would spend together. Also, Steve enjoyed surprising Sally with spontaneous visits to her office and romantic dates.

A few years later, I saw Sally and Steve at a Dallas Stars hockey game. I was there with our son, Adam. Their smiles and sparkling eyes in the midst of a loud, rough, and exciting hockey game were wonderful to see. I was delighted to hear Steve say, "We have a fantastic marriage." Sally, beaming, hugged him like a schoolgirl.

Unless we intentionally and committedly change negative behaviors from our family of origin, we tend to carry them into our own intimate relationships. Sally and Steve's story illustrates this. They thought their attitudes and behaviors toward each other were normal and acceptable. Their relationship was only surviving when they came to therapy. They soon realized their destructive attitudes and behaviors were killing their relationship. And they were willing to make the necessary changes to develop their own unique, loving relationship.

Do Friends and Peers Affect Whom We Marry?

In addition to parental influence, another influence on mate selection and relationship development to consider is the broader social network that branches out from our parents. This network may include grandparents, siblings, or other relatives. For some people, their extended family provides a significant impact on their lives.

The developmental experience of leaving one's family, however, is usually accompanied by the expanding influence of friends and peers. In a society in which parents have a decreasing impact on mate selection, have peers become the primary external influence concerning who will marry whom?

Participants in my study indicated that approval by parents and friends is only "somewhat important" in relationship development. Yet, it was clear that parental approval was *more* important than peer approval throughout the couples' relationship.

The importance of parental approval changes during the course of the relationship. My study shows parental approval is of *little* importance when couples first meet, becomes *more* important during their courtship, is *most* important when they get married, and *lessens* somewhat in importance in later years.

A question I ask premarital couples is: "How do your parents feel about your getting married?" This is not meant to imply that parents must approve of the marriage. But their approval or disapproval of a couple's relationship can significantly affect all the relationships involved, as well as individual feelings. The same could be said about friends being for or against a relationship. True, the relationship belongs to the couple. But what is also true is that most of us do not live in a vacuum. We live in a social context with people, especially parents and friends, who are important to us.

Couples' social networks may serve as influences regarding the acceleration or deceleration of a relationship. Family and friends are not usually determiners of courtship progress.

Couples in my study rated discussing their families of origin higher during courtship than at any other time in their relationship. While courting, couples are being introduced to the family and friends. As couples become more committed to the relationship, each person must find ways to deal with and/or relate to these outside influences. Couples rated getting along with each others' families as increasingly important throughout the relationship process.

If you marry, you also marry your partner's family. There may only be a bride and groom perched atop your wedding cake, but usually a lot of people attend the wedding ceremony, and many of these people will be a part of your marriage. Often these people are supportive and loving. Sometimes they may be negative or distant. Being able to openly discuss your families, and to get along with each others' families, is more important to couples than parental approval of the relationship.

How Couples Deal With Outside Influences

While the opinions of family and friends matter, how couples decide to deal with outside opinions will affect their relationship more. This does not mean couples necessarily need to have a united front against family members, except in extreme circumstances. It is more important for couples to be aware of each others' families so that they can discuss and make joint decisions about everything, from how they handle holiday visits to a parent's intrusive behavior.

As history evolved and society changed, so did the dominance of parents and the development of romantic love in mate selection. Whether the "jungle" was a hostile and beastly environment, a culture where marriages were arranged by parents, or a mysterious romantic love that brought people to the altar with parents and friends in the background, couples have always been seeking ways to survive and thrive in mate selection.

What Kind of Jungle Did You Come From?

To successfully survive and thrive in our present and future jungles, it is extremely important for all of us to understand and deal with the jungles we and our potential mates have come from. Your jungle may have been a healthy, loving, supportive, and secure environment. Or your jungle may have been a volatile, distant, controlling, or unpredictable environment. Is there a history in your jungle of addiction, abuse, depression, or emotional instability?

How you deal with your past and your family not only affects your individual life, it also affects how you deal with mate selection and relationship development. If you are in a relationship, the same is true for your partner and your relationship with his or her jungle.

The Beginning of Your Thriving Relationship

It is truly a jungle out there. Finding and being a good mate, developing a healthy relationship, and having a rewarding and lasting marriage are not easy tasks. We bring our own jungles to, and into, relationships. To be aware of these jungles and their effects upon us and others is critically important for our own well-being and the well-being of our relationships—especially our intimate relationships.

In our culture and in this time in Western history, we can choose mates and develop relationships without parental prearrangement. And we can do so with a host of jungle experiences. We also have the opportunity and power to be healthier people and have better relationships. This is not the end. It is the beginning of having a fulfilling, lifetime marriage.

Instead of being like Ugh and Umm, who simpl. in their jungle, I invite you to be aware of, explore, and successfully survive your past jungle and your mate's past jungle. That survival will allow the two of you to start down the path to thriving in a lush, resourceful, harmonious, love-filled garden.

Take some time to look at your past and at your family or families. To help you successfully survive and thrive in mate selection, or in a developing relationship or in marriage, write and verbalize responses to each of the following questions which apply to you and your situation. If you are in a relationship, do this as a sharing exercise.

Family of Origin Exercise

1. Briefly describe your mother and/or maternal figures when you were growing up. You may have had stepmothers, grandmothers or other significant females who were maternal figures.
2. Briefly describe your past and present relationship with the above. You may use some of the words from the previous answer which describe your jungle: loving, controlling, and so forth.
3. Briefly describe how you felt in the past and currently feel in the above relationship(s). Use "feeling" words such as "safe," "scared," "uncomfortable," "loved."
4. From these experiences and feelings, briefly describe what conclusions you came to and/or decisions you made about: 1) yourself, 2) that relationship, 3) future relationships. Such conclusions are things like: "I am a good person," "I can never please you," "I will never get close to anyone."
5. Briefly describe your father and/or father figures when

you were growing up.
6. Briefly describe your past and present relationship with your father and/or father figures.
7. Briefly describe how you felt in the past and currently feel in your relationship(s) with your father and/or father figures.
8. From these experiences and feelings, briefly describe what conclusions you came to and/or decisions you made about: 1) yourself, 2) that relationship, 3) future relationships.
9. If you are in a relationship, describe how you and how your partner are similar to your mother and father, and how you are different from them.
10. Describe your parents' marriage(s).
11. If you are in a relationship, this is a good time to take turns so the other person can share responses to the above questions.
12. Do you or your family have a history of addiction, abuse, depression, or emotional instability? If so, be sure you address these issues.
13. Do you or your family have a history of volatile, distant, or controlling behavior? If so, be sure you deal with these issues.
14. Are there other personal or relationship issues from your past, or from your families, which are important for you to address and discuss with your mate?
15. Considering your responses to the above questions, what are important issues for you to address regarding mate selection and/or a surviving and thriving relationship?
16. Discuss how your family shared love, celebrated, and supported each other.
17. What have you done? What are you doing? What will

you do to successfully address these issues for your own well-being and for the well-being of your relationship with your partner?

Draw a Picture of Your Family

An additional exercise which I often find useful is for individuals or couples to draw pictures of their families. Depict a time or a scene from your childhood. This is not an art assignment, but a graphic way to describe families. It is an insightful way to look at your own family and each other's families for awareness and understanding. Have fun drawing, sharing, and discussing. You may also discuss how you wish your families had been different. And then it is *most important* for you to discuss how you want your present family to be.

PART TWO:
ATTRACTION! ATTRACTION!

Chapter 2
Birds of a Feather or Opposites?

While my wife and I were at the Orlando airport waiting for our flight home to Dallas, I was talking with an acquaintance of my wife about the book I was writing. This book. "My husband and I have been married 12 years and we are very different," she stated, then added, "I think opposites attract. Do you?"

A friend of mine was explaining to me how he and his wife are very similar. Both are Jewish. From the same hometown. They went to the same university. They both have graduate degrees. He told me he thought their similarities were a key ingredient to their good marriage.

Both my wife's friend and my friend are right...for them.

In the complex process of mate selection, relationship development, and marriage, there are many factors which contribute to our coupling with another. As we enter the relationship jungle, some *differences* in manly Ugh and womanly Umm are intriguing and attractive. Likewise, some *similarities* are familiar and reassuring.

Some of the "givens" we bring into the relationship jungle are seven sociocultural factors: race or ethnic origin, education level, religious background, work or career, family, socioeconomic background, and age. Let's examine the importance of both differences and similarities as they relate to sociocultural factors in mate selection and marriage.

The French have the popular saying, *vive la différence*—"long live the difference." I have a saying: "Opposites often attract–they just have a hard time living with each other." Some couples come in differing combinations. Hispanic and Asian. Well-educated and little-educated. Jew and Christian. Laborer and manager. Wealthy and poor. Ages 38 and 23. While these differences may add spice, variety, and growth potential for couples, they may also present challenges or obstacles which need to be addressed.

Similarities

"Birds of a feather flock together" is an old English proverb which illustrates the thinking of similarity theory. A vast amount of research has been carried out by social psychologists and demographers to discover how similarity accounts for friendship, courtship, and marriage. Various sociocultural studies regarding marital choice have addressed such similarity variables as age, ethnicity, religion, birth order, education, intelligence, personality traits, physical attractiveness, propinquity (nearness or proximity), values, and socioeconomic factors. These variables, however, seem to relate more to the creation of a pool of marital "candidates" rather than to actual mate selection. The variables create possibilities for mate selection. *Actual mate selection must be based on more than these similarity variables*.

Sociocultural Factors

At the front door of a relationship are factors we bring with us over which we have no control. In spite of hair coloring, plastic surgery, or a youthful or very mature attitude, we are the age we are because we were born on a particular day in a certain year. Likewise, our race or ethnic origin and family and socioeconomic background are parts of our inheritance.

We may pay little attention to these factors as we go through our daily lives, only thinking about them when we fill out information forms. Or we may be very sensitive to them. No matter what level of attention we give these factors, these are only a few of the numerous traits we carry by which we may be known, accepted, or judged. These are also factors which, intentionally or unintentionally, consciously or unconsciously, affect mate selection, relationship development, and marriage.

Race or Ethnic Origin

An array of scientists concludes we all descended from Umm and her forebears many years ago. All of us Homo sapiens carry a particular type of DNA that has been passed through each generation. We are all more similar than we are different. But among the differences which have often segregated us geographically, culturally, and personally, has been our race or ethnic origin. This is one of those traits we inherit from the time the sperm and egg unite—and it affects how we couple as mates. Some people are especially attracted to persons of different ethnic origins. Others may give little consideration to this factor. Still others are primarily or *only* attracted to persons of similar or the same ethnic origin.

My study was primarily composed of persons who listed their ethnicity as Caucasian. Others in the study were African American, Hispanic, Asian American, and Native American. Most Caucasians had married Caucasians. Most African Americans had married African Americans. Most Hispanics, Asian Americans, and Native Americans had married within their own ethnicity. Some people in all these groups married outside their ethnicity, but most had married within.

Of the seven items in my study which related to sociocultural factors, participants ranked their spouse's race or ethnic origin as *the most important*. One can conclude that for most people, ethnicity is a significant factor at the beginning of the filtering process of a relationship. That process may lead to marriage. However, as we become a more culturally diverse and integrated society, as well as a more global community, marriages between different ethnicities may increase. While couples from the same racial or ethnic origin have one less issue to overcome, couples from different racial or ethnic origins must address this issue with full awareness of implications for themselves, for their families, and for their children.

Sue and Richard are a good example of a couple who addressed this issue. Sue is from Malaysia. Richard is from Iowa. They met at a university religious group's social, and immediately engaged in an animated conversation about each other's different backgrounds.

When I met with them for pre-premarital counseling, Richard said he was attracted by Sue's beauty and curious nature. Her flashing dark eyes and gentle voice warmed his heart. Sue revealed she was initially attracted by Richard's kind manner and interest in her. His many questions about Malaysia and her background caused her to feel he cared about her.

While their relationship had developed well—and their friends thought they were "just meant for each other"—their primary concern was how their families would deal with their ethnic and cultural differences. Richard explained his parents had voiced their concern about his dating someone "so different." Sue declared her concern was that her parents would be upset because this blue-eyed, blond man from Iowa would keep her from returning to her homeland. Both Sue and Richard made a list of the concerns their parents might have and discussed how they might most effectively address these issues with them.

Sue and Richard wrote letters to their parents which included their possible concerns and each asked for their reply. Both sets of parents replied and both added a few more concerns. Sue's parents feared that she would lose the traditions of her native culture and that they would never see their grandchildren. Richard's dad admitted it was difficult for him to imagine "half-Malaysian grandchildren" carrying on their German family name. His mom worried that Richard would want to live in Malaysia.

Sue and Richard addressed each concern. Each wrote letters to the other's parents and followed with phone calls. They discovered that the more information they shared with their own and each other's parents, the more their differences diminished as their similarities were enhanced.

Sue and Richard were of similar age, education level, and religious beliefs. By the time Sue met Richard's family in Iowa and Richard and Sue met her family, who flew from Malaysia to California, numerous concerns had been addressed and calmed.

Sue and Richard have been married 15 years and have two children. They now live in California where Sue's aunt, uncle, and three cousins live. Sue and Richard and their children visit Iowa once or twice a year, and they travel to Malaysia about every three years. This couple's effectiveness in dealing with different racial and ethnic origins included their commitment to intentionally and sensitively address their own and their families' concerns. They also communicated positively and lovingly with their own families and with each other's families, and they built on their similarities, such as education and beliefs.

The Age Factor

We've established that race or ethnic origin is very important to most couples who marry. Is age that important? The findings from my study reveal different views. If we rank the seven items associated with sociocultural factors, it ranks last in importance. However, analysis of the demographic data reveals some intriguing information.

My study's participants covered a wide range of ages when they married—from 18 to 37 for males and 13 to 38 for females. Most males married between the ages of 22 and 25. Most females wed between the ages of 20 and 23. The overall average age for men at their time of marriage was 24.5 years, 22.9 years for women.

In most cases, the ages of individuals marrying were within three years of each other. *Although study participants ranked the importance of age of their spouse near the bottom of 36 items, the demographic data indicate that age is a significant factor for marriage candidates.*

There is a *great* likelihood that you will marry, or are married to, a person within three years of your own age. Statistically, there is an *overwhelming* likelihood people marry within a five-year range. There are, of course, exceptions. Even so, as unimportant as people may say age is for marriage, similar age seems to be a significant marriage factor for most people *who have married only once.*

An example of a similar-aged couple is John and Ethel. They were born only three months apart. I visited this couple a number of times in their home in the late '70s, while I was the minister of pastoral care and counseling at a large suburban church. John and Ethel had been married more than 50 years and had no children. John had had a stroke and was confined to their home. Ethel faithfully and lovingly cared for him.

During a visit, I asked them how they met. John chuckled, and began to slowly tell the story. He drooled as he spoke. He explained that he and a friend were driving on an unpaved road in a Model A Ford when they saw two young women walking in the same direction in front of them. As they neared the women, John turned to his friend, who was driving the car, and asked him if he noticed the young woman on the right. John paused, and looked at me with a twinkle in his eye. "I told my friend I was going to marry that girl—and I hadn't even seen the front of her!" John recalled. He laughed until he began to cough.

Ethel moved close to her husband and calmed him. While standing beside him, she lovingly brushed his hair back with her hand. Her voice was softly confident, "We married three months later and we've had a wonderful marriage."

A year after I started visiting John and Ethel, I conducted their funeral. They died about 24 hours apart. John died of a stroke, Ethel from a heart attack.

I will never forget them, especially their story of devotion to each other and their genuine love. They were 17 when they married. I do not recommend getting married at 17, even if you and the one you care about are the same age. It is only one factor of similarity. Nor do I recommend instantly deciding to marry someone because his or her backside caught your attention. And I would strongly caution against marrying after only three months of courtship.

John and Ethel were an exception to these guidelines. Their story comes from a different era and, quite frankly, they were a wonderfully extraordinary couple.

Length of Courtship

The time of Model A Fords, leisurely walks down unpaved roads, and three-month courtships was one quite different from today's traffic jams, high divorce rates, and extended years seeking an education. Many changes over the decades have affected mate selection, courtship, and marriage.

One factor which affects age at the time of marriage is the length of courtship. Couples in my study had courtships which ranged from six months to 13 years. The courtships of most couples was between 18 months and two and one-half years. The average length of courtship of the 108 couples was 28.5 months.

During the '70s and '80s, there was a dramatic shift in courtship length compared to that of the '50s and '60s. Couples who married in the '50s and '60s courted an average of 26-27 months. Couples who married in the '70s courted an average of almost 33 months. Those married in the '80s courted an average of about 30 months. These differences may be associated with the phenomenon of more couples living together before they marry.

Couples who married during the '90s had an average courtship of approximately 26 months—similar to couples who married in the '50s. However, in the '90s, more and more couples did not marry until after the age of 25. One factor associated with this trend is the amount of time spent in formal education before marriage. This factor is especially true for women, who have consistently increased their level of education over the decades.

One question I ask couples who come for marital or premarital counseling is "How long was your courtship?" If they courted only a few months, I ask them, "Why were you in such a hurry to get married?" If they courted several years, I ask, "Why did you wait so long?"

I don't think there is a best length for courtship. Courtship is, however, that time when couples can *really* get to know each other well. It is the time they can use to answer crucial questions. How do they, as a couple, deal with school or work situations? How do they deal with family and friends? What are their interests and hobbies? How do they deal with stress? What are their bad habits? How well do they treat each other? How controlling, insecure, or jealous are they? How faithful and committed are they? What are their values and religious beliefs? What is truly important to them?

A good motto for courtship is "Let time be your friend." Getting to know each other in various situations over time can provide a solid foundation for a strong relationship. The knowledge gained about each other during a lengthy courtship will help couples know if they really want to spend a lifetime with each other.

More and more, I meet with couples for pre-premarital counseling. These are couples who are considering getting married. They are in love, but they have some relationship issues which concern them. Or they may want to confirm that they are compatible with each other. These sessions are generally extremely helpful for these couples. They are not under the pressure of a public engagement or wedding plans. Such opportunities were unheard of in John and Ethel's time.

In the relationship jungles we live in today, a few sessions of pre-premarital counseling may help couples resolve important issues. They may be able to confirm the healthiness of their relationship and help it to grow. Or they may decide to end a relationship that may be inherently unhealthy or beset with problems that cannot be resolved. And they can do that without having to inform everyone sent an invitation that the wedding is off.

If you are considering getting married, this is an excellent time to discuss your relationship with a professional trained and experienced in this area. If you are already planning the details of your wedding, I urge you to do more than decide on the type of cake you want. Investing in premarital counseling will most assuredly help your marriage last a lot longer than any element of the ceremony.

Is Education Important?

In our society education tends to segregate us by age. Most people will spend a number of years in school with people in the same age group. Many couples will also meet while in school.

My wife and I met in February 1971. We were in the cafeteria at Southern Methodist University. I was in the theology school and Kathleen was in the music school. A mutual friend introduced us during the lunch hour.

Kathleen had big, beautiful brown eyes, dark, waist-length hair and a friendly smile. Our mutual friend, Raynelle, playfully introduced Kathleen by saying "Terry, this is my friend, umm—Helen." Although I quickly learned her real name, I continued to call Kathleen "Helen" until I met her parents several months later. During the summer break, I wrote letters to her in Tulsa addressed to "Helen of Tulsa." She and I still flirtingly comment when she is in a "Helen of a mood." Believe me, Kathleen was by far the best thing I ever found in that cafeteria.

Education played a key role in my study. A majority of the participants had one or more college degrees. Over 90 percent had at least some college. While women rated the education level of their spouse as being very important, both men and women indicated it was a critical factor for mate selection and relationship development.

What does this mean? When viewed as a sociocultural factor, most people believe education is important. Most parents want their children to receive good educations and most adults also want to have a high level of education. Education is a value rated highly in our society. A similarity in relationships is established simply by being together in school or having a like level of education.

Although the value of education is very generalized, a more relational factor associated with education is that it provides both academic and social environments which affect how people think and communicate. We've all heard the classic stories of the woman who works to put her husband through medical school or the man who works to put his wife through law school, and after graduation the marriages end in divorce. How many years a person spends in school may not be the crucial factor—it's how the person thinks and communicates that affects a couple's relationship progress.

When an educational difference may be an issue for one or both members of the couple, it is absolutely essential for the couple to discuss this difference. Only then can they agree on how to bridge the education gap for the sake of their relationship.

That bridge can take many forms.

One man who had "barely gotten out of high school" married a woman with a master's degree. He worked increasingly more challenging crossword puzzles and became involved in a public speaking organization. Both helped him to feel more confident; he even became more successful professionally.

A woman who had dropped out of college to help her husband through medical school returned to college. She is now a successful child therapist.

There is no doubt that education affects mate selection and marriage. How couples deal with this factor can be very important to their relationship development.

Religious Background

There were three questions associated with religion in my

study. One was about religious background. Another was about comparing values and religious beliefs. The third asked about how the couple practiced their values or religious beliefs. The focus in this section will address the religious *background* issue.

Participants in my study were primarily Protestants, with representation from other faiths including Roman Catholics, Jews, Pentacostals, Buddhists, and others. There were also several participants who indicated no religious preference.

The majority of couples had the same religious background, indicating the importance of this factor. It is clear that religious background, or lack thereof, can be a very important factor in relationships. For some couples, a similar religious affiliation was a prerequisite for a dating relationship. Religious groups are also places where couples meet, lending weight to the proverbial "birds of a feather flock together" axiom for mate selection.

The religious background factor was important throughout the relationship, but most important when couples married. When couples begin to think seriously about getting married, religious backgrounds often take on an increased importance.

An Ill-Fated Relationship

Peter came from a strict Roman Catholic background. Kathy came from a Southern Baptist background. They met at a university fraternity-sorority party and were immediately attracted to each other. Within a few weeks, they were dating each other exclusively. Also, while away from their families, they did not actively participate in religious services and rarely discussed religion.

After dating for eight months in an increasingly serious relationship, Peter and Kathy were apart during the summer break. While home with their families, they each had several conversations with their parents about their particular faiths.

Peter went to visit Kathy during the Fourth of July weekend. The couple discussed the religious background issue more fully. They talked about what it would mean if they had children and in which faith their children should be reared.

Throughout that summer, Peter attended mass at his home church regularly. He also visited with a priest two times about the different religious backgrounds he and Kathy had. Peter reported that the priest did not really give him advice. He said that the priest explained several differences and similarities between the faiths, and said he would pray for Peter and Kathy to make a good decision. Being somewhat independent, Peter appreciated the priest's not telling him what to do. However, Peter began to more seriously consider the possibility that the religious differences between him and Kathy might become a significant problem.

Throughout the summer, Kathy talked with her parents about the faith issues. She also met with her pastor. Her pastor discussed various theological issues with Kathy and he asked her to prayerfully consider these matters. She struggled with them during her solitary walks each evening.

Peter and Kathy discussed their religious beliefs during their frequent phone conversations that summer. Both Peter and Kathy became increasingly frustrated with their inability to agree about several key beliefs.

When they returned to school for their senior year, Peter and Kathy came to me as a neutral third party to help them examine their faith differences. Kathy told me in a session with Peter that she and her mother had several talks about the Roman Catholic faith. She said she was not sure she could accept some of the religion's beliefs. In the same session, Peter said he and his parents had several conversations about Kathy's religious beliefs.

Peter and Kathy spent the next three months seriously examining and exploring their own and each other's religious beliefs and their relationship. Kathy lamented, "It just doesn't seem fair that our religious backgrounds should be a cause for problems." Peter said, "When looked at from one perspective, our spiritual and faith beliefs are so similar. Yet, from another perspective, our religious backgrounds and beliefs are such that we just can't agree or negotiate a workable solution."

The couple concluded that the differences in their religious beliefs were ones they could not agree upon. They wanted to remain friends but found it too painful. They decided to end their relationship so they could get on with their lives.

As heart-wrenching as this experience was for Peter and Kathy, they realized they had learned a lot about themselves as individuals. In addition, they also learned more about their own religious beliefs and each other's religious beliefs. They found comfort in the knowledge they had understood this *before* they married.

A Relationship That Worked

Christy was a 27-year-old critical care nurse who came from a long line of "Georgia Methodists." Joel was a 30-year-old medical resident who smilingly described his family as "long-time New York Jews." They had met while working at a large medical facility. They were contemplating marriage when they came to me for pre-premarital counseling.

Over the next several months, Christy and Joel focused their attention upon their similarities as special human beings who connected on a deep spiritual level. They also addressed the important issues of their differences in religious beliefs, including how to deal with religious holidays and how they would rear children.

They were embraced by each other's families and they shared with their parents how they wanted to deal with the differences presented by their religious beliefs. Joel commented, "Christy and I believe we are bright people who love each other. We are so committed to each other that our parents know better than to try to talk us out of it." Christy added, "Our respect for each other enables us to address an issue that was a 'first' for our families." She said their families accepted them because they saw how good they were for, and to, each other.

Joel and Christy are exceptionally open people. Their relationship worked for them. Their wedding was a true celebration and coming together of Northerner and Southerner, Jew and Christian, two loving families, and two special individuals. They are now a dynamite couple who have two dynamite children. They are teaching their children about their Judeo-Christian heritage.

Religious Differences and Similarities

As I mentioned earlier, I do not do "cookie-cutter" therapy because I do not see "cookie-cutter" people. Kathy and Peter and Christy and Joel are examples. If you are considering marrying a person from a different faith, this is an important issue for you to examine, discuss, address, and pray about. If you are married to a person from a different faith, how you deal with this issue is critical. In Chapter 5, some ways to deal with religious and other differences are discussed.

Work or Career

The most significant difference between men's and women's scores in my study concerned their spouses' work or career.

From their first meeting, through their courtship, to their getting married and to the present time in their marriage, their spouses' work or career was increasingly important to women. As the relationship develops, women like a man who has a job or career. There was no significant difference in these scores over the decades from the '40s to the '90s. *This finding indicates that women value a mate or potential mate who has economic promise and stability.*

Although more and more women are in the work force, women continue to place significantly more emphasis on the spouse's work or career than do men. This may be a sign of sexism or just the way things are. Whatever the reasons, a 25-year-old single woman in one of my seminars very succinctly summarized the viewpoint of many of the adult women in my study. "Unless a man has a job, I won't go out with him," she declared.

Men in my study placed much less emphasis on their mate's career or work. However, those who married during the '80s and '90s indicated the increasing importance of this issue. This is an indication of a trend of men being more aware of and valuing women's careers in the context of their relationship.

Another item in my study associated with work or career concerned couples discussing their career goals. There was only a slight difference between men's and women's scores on this item. Both men and women indicated it was an increasingly important issue for their discussion, but women always rated discussing career goals higher than men.

The work/career jungle in which many individuals and couples operate is not always a very stable environment. Frequent job losses or inability to make a living affect a person's self-esteem and bank account. Inevitably, these things also have an impact on an intimate relationship. Conversely, having a positive career path or economic security can be a very important factor for relationship stability. That doesn't mean that a good job is the key to dating or to keeping a marriage going. But the instability of not having a job can seriously strain any relationship.

Family and Socioeconomic Backgrounds

In the first chapter we looked at the family jungles we come from. The emphasis then was on the people in the family jungle and their relationships. An item associated with the family jungle is the socioeconomic background. Again, women rated these items of family and socioeconomic backgrounds as much more important than men. A man in one of my seminars made an interesting comment about these factors. He said, "Although my socioeconomic background affects me, I have been able to overcome it and achieve a lot in my 36 years. In some ways, I have overcome my family background, but my wife and I must still deal with my family."

The families and socioeconomic backgrounds from which we come may affect everything: *Our experiences and concepts of privilege and poverty. Family closeness and distance. Saving and spending. Pride and prejudice. Drinking alcohol and tee-totaling. Work and leisure. Letting it all hang out. Keeping a stiff upper lip.* The similarities and differences about these and a host of other factors which come from our family and socioeconomic backgrounds may provide a lifetime of jungle fodder for couples to address.

In the complex process of mate selection, relationship development, and marriage, the combination of sociocultural similarities and differences can bring us closer together or separate us. Sociocultural factors may be at the front door of couples getting together, consciously or unconsciously—and they may remain issues to be dealt with over the lifetime of the relatione one's mind these kinds of thoughts may be filtering potential mates or affecting our relationships:

We are the same or different race or ethnicity.

He/she is too old/young for me.

If only we had courted longer.

Why is he/she so scared to get married?

There's just too much difference in our schooling.

I'm so glad our religious beliefs are similar.

Could my parents handle me marrying outside their faith?

If only he/she had a job.

Does he/she think I will support him/her forever?

Our families will just love each other.

You really do marry their family.

Whatever your marital status or stage in a relationship, it is important to be aware of the factors from your sociocultural jungles which you bring to and into a relationship. The following exercises will help you, or you and your partner, to examine and discuss these factors which are so important for relationship development.

Sociocultural Background Exercise

1. How is your and/or your partner's race or ethnic origin an issue regarding your relationship?
2. How does your age similarity or difference affect your relationship?
3. What are your thoughts or concerns about the length of your courtship?
4. What are your thoughts or concerns about your education levels?
5. How do the differences and similarities in your religious backgrounds affect your relationship?
6. What are your thoughts or concerns about work or career

as they relate to your relationship?
7. How do the similarities and differences of your family backgrounds affect your relationship?
8. How do the similarities and differences of your socioeconomic backgrounds affect your relationship?
9. Creatively and positively address ways to build on your similarities and deal with your differences.

Chapter 3
I Like Your Mind, Love Your Body

Whenever I ask a couple what they thought of each other when they first met, they usually smile as this vivid memory jumps clearly into focus in their minds. Whether their meeting was 50 days or 50 years ago, both men and women can usually remember that first sensation. This is not necessarily love at first sight, but it is *attraction at first sight.* For a relationship to begin, that attraction is the first step. Let's look at the issue of attraction, which may happen at the first meeting and which continues to be an important quality for the lifetime of the marriage.

What Attracts Men?

According to the men in my study, at the top of the attraction meter are four items: 1) physical attraction to my spouse, 2) my spouse's physical attractiveness, 3) my spouse's sexual attractiveness, and 4) my spouse's personality characteristics.

Men may not always be the most feeling creatures on the planet, but a feeling which will really get their attention is physical attraction to a woman. If men have at least fair eyesight, there is a great likelihood that their optic nerves will send an immediate message to the attraction part of the brain. That part will react with flashing red lights: "*Physical Attraction! Physical Attraction!*"

Some men are *always* scoping out the possibilities, while others may be more discriminating. Whatever their level of testosterone, desire, interest, or awareness may be, physical attraction really begins in the eyes of the male beholder and is activated by the presence of a particular type of female. Men described their attraction feelings as "powerful"... "int ense"..."exciting"..."arousing"..."rare"..."wow"..."she's sexy" and "umm."

Closely associated with the physical attraction sparked in the man is the woman's physical attractiveness. Basically, physical attractiveness for both men and women includes physical traits or qualities they notice and find to be pleasing to the eye. Physical attraction is the *internal excitement* one has in response to the physical attractiveness of the other person. Men rated these items as being almost identical in importance.

Some women may be discouraged that most men may not be initially attracted by their intelligence, accomplishments, personality traits, or inner beauty. Although the men in my study were highly educated, the woman's physical attractiveness was rated as very important and seemed to activate their level of interest.

What kinds of traits do men find attractive? The men responded with: "her beauty"..."her face"..."her figure"..."her posture and the way she carried herself"..."her eyes"..."her smile"..."her hair"..."her gracefulness"..."her legs"..."her grooming" and "the way she dressed." These may seem to be superficial qualities, but the primary sense the male seems to employ at this time is sight.

Closely associated with physical attraction and physical attractiveness is sexual attractiveness. While descriptions of physical attractiveness were more general and observational, descriptions of sexual attractiveness were more specific and personal. Some responses are: "she has a great body"..."her beautiful face"..."her shapely legs"..."her breasts"..."her body language"..."comfortable with her body"..."her long hair"..."beautiful smile"..."a great tan"..."her voice" and "short skirt."

While human development may have evolved over the ages, the physical or biological processes are the first sources of attraction for most men. It just seems that is how we were created. The combination of the woman's physical and sexual attractiveness results in physical attraction, possibly before a single word is ever spoken.

In fairness to men, the importance of the woman's personality characteristics in their first meeting were rated almost equally with her sexual attractiveness. Key personality qualities include: "She was so nice"..."She was a lot of fun"..."She had a great personality"..."She had a good sense of humor"..."We talked a lot"..."She was affectionate"..."She was really smart" and "She laughed at my jokes."

So, for men, physical attraction usually begins as a visual experience when they see a woman they find to be physically and sexually enticing. The attraction is then developed by the woman's personality characteristics and the experiences they have together. With the combination of these qualities in place, many men reported, "I definitely wanted to see her again."

What Attracts Women?

The highest rated item—by far—revealed by women regarding what was most important about their spouses at their first meeting was that spouse's personality characteristics. From the outset, women seem to be much more oriented to what they experience *from* and *in* a relationship with the man. This is in stark contrast to the man's primary visual orientation.

Men, do you really want to know what women find attractive in a man and what is important in a mate? Here's what women said were essential to a good start: "He seemed nice"... "He was pleasant"..."He was kind"..."He made me laugh"..."He had a good sense of humor"..."He seemed confident"..."He was considerate and polite"..."He was friendly"..."He had a positive attitude"..."He could talk and listen"..."He seemed to know what he wanted"..."He seemed ambitious" and "I felt comfortable with him."

The items women ranked next in importance in their first meeting was the man's intelligence. These women in my study described this quality in several ways, including "He was intelligent"..."He was smart"..."He was quick"..."He was really sharp" and "I liked the way he talked and our conversations." Because the women were well-educated and the men they married were well-educated, intelligence *must* be an attractive quality to many women.

Physical attraction, sexual attractiveness, and physical attractiveness were rated by women somewhat lower than personality and intelligence. All three were rated as having almost equal importance. In fact, the descriptions associated with each quality frequently overlapped. Once she "likes" the man, physical attraction, sexual attractiveness, and physical attractiveness may be more important to a woman. Descriptions associated with physical attraction included "I felt very comfortable with him"..."I just really liked him"..."I had this warm feeling with him"..."He sort of reminded me of my dad"..."I wanted to get to know him better" and "I thought, umm, he might be the one for me."

Women described the man's sexual attractiveness and physical attractiveness similarly—"I thought he was very handsome"..."I really liked his eyes"..."I felt very comfortable with him"..."I liked his smile and warm manner"..."He was clean- cut"..."He was dressed nicely"..."I liked the way he held my hand"..."He had a nice body" and "He was really cute."

Don't misunderstand. The above information is not intended to suggest that a woman may not be initially attracted to a man's physical appearance or sexual attractiveness. What the study's findings indicate are that, in a ranking of importance in their initial meeting, women placed more importance on the personality characteristics and intelligence than on physical attraction, sexual attractiveness, or physical attractiveness. So, for most women, physical attraction is a combination of the man's personality characteristics and intelligence combined with physical and sexual attractiveness.

As a therapist, I listen to what people *do not* say as well as what they *do* say. People who have been married only one time did not usually say they got married to get out of a bad home situation or because they thought the other person needed him or her or because they thought their mates would change after they married. All of us bring our jungles with us, but *escaping, rescuing, and unrealistic expectations were not among the primary reasons for marriage*.

Although some women may be initially attracted to Ugh's cute butt, muscular arms, great legs, or hairy chest, these do not seem to be the most important qualities for mate selection and lifetime relationships in today's jungle. So, guys, whether you are single, dating, or married, if you really want a great relationship with a woman, you would do well to spend as much time working on developing good personality characteristics, relationship qualities, and intelligence as you do working on your body to develop rippling pecs.

Bottom line: Men tend to like women's minds and love their bodies. Women tend to love men's minds and like their bodies. Although the order of priorities may be somewhat different, this does not have to be a problem for couples if they experience mutual fulfillment in the relationship.

The Continuing Importance of Attraction

Findings from my study indicate that attraction qualities *initially experienced in the couple's first meeting* are important for the *ongoing development of the relationship*. Men reported that attraction peaked during courtship and women reported that attraction peaked when they got married. Although attraction qualities dropped in ranking during the continuation of the relationship, the various attraction qualities remained important throughout the marriage.

As the relationship develops and couples come to like, and love, each other more, one's partner is viewed as even more attractive. While exploring or intentionally trying to develop a relationship, both men and women usually put their best feet forward. The woman may make extra attempts to look her best, while the man may try to both look good and have pleasing personality and relationship qualities.

From the time a couple is engaged and gets married, they often have more photographs taken of them than any other time in their lives. They want to look their best. For some men, their wedding is the first and, possibly, only time they will ever wear formal attire. Unless they are celebrities, most women will spend more time—and money—on their personal appearance and dress for their wedding than for any other occasion in their lives. Brides and grooms want to look great for each other. And for all of those wedding pictures people may admire for generations.

Busy schedules with careers and child-rearing take much time and effort for many years for most couples. One of my seminar topics which addresses this subject is: *How to be Married, Have Children, and Stay Sane*. Earning enough money, being an involved parent, and juggling activities are huge responsibilities. Even so, both husbands and wives report that attraction remains important for a marriage to survive and thrive during those hectic years.

Years beyond the wedding, most older couples continue to find attraction an important quality. As we'll discuss in future chapters, some of these qualities may shift in importance, but for some couples attraction is special.

Henry and Elsie

Henry and Elsie are in their 70s and are very active. Henry plays golf as often as possible. He can shoot his age for the first time in his life, he says with genuine pride. Elsie is active in church and community activities. She makes "little do-dads" for her great-grandchildren.

Recently, during a visit with the couple, Henry remarked to me that Elsie is still the prettiest girl he has ever seen. He said she is as pretty as the first time he met her at a church social. Elsie responded with a girlish smile that belied her age, as she gushed, "Oh, Henry, you don't know what you're talking about." Then, she added, with strong conviction, "Henry is a kinder man now than he's ever been. And he looks better than a lot of men half his age."

With a twinkle in his eyes and a head nod for emphasis, Henry communicated clearly the attraction he has for his wife, "When you have a wife who looks this good after all these years—and has that special sparkle in her amber eyes—a man would be crazy to not think he is very, very lucky."

With certainty in her voice and that girlish smile, Elsie communicated clearly the attraction she has for her husband. "I just love his white hair, his handsome face, and the way he still winks at me with his baby blue eyes."

Henry and Elsie take great pride in presenting the best selves they can to each other. Elsie whispered, "I always knew Henry thought I was pretty. And I didn't want to do *anything* to change his mind."

Henry almost apologetically said, "After we were married for a while, I was not as kind to Elsie as I should have been." Then, he added, "The good Lord has given me a lot of years to be kind to her—like I was when we courted."

Attraction is different things for different people from different jungles. Ugh found Umm's curvy, strong, and somewhat hairy body attractive. Umm thought Ugh's cute face with a slanted forehead and his strong, hairy body were attractive.

The following exercise will help you address questions regarding attraction, no matter what your relationship status is. Enjoy it.

Attraction Exercise

1. What personality characteristics are important to you in your mate or potential mate?
2. If you are married or in a relationship, what personality characteristics did you initially find attractive about your partner?
3. What did you, and what do you now find, to be attractive physical qualities in a mate?
4. Describe what physical attraction is and/or was for you.
5. Describe what sexual attractiveness is and/or was for you.
6. If you are married or in a relationship, what can you and your partner do to cause your attraction to thrive?

PART THREE:
FROM ROMANCE TO COMMITMENT

Chapter 4
Romance: The Emotional Orgasm

When couples are really attracted to each other, the feelings of desire, passion, and compassion may become so strong that they create a focus and intensity which may be described as love. More accurately, this intensity might be termed romance. This is an experience which usually feels *so good* that the couple wants to be with each other and close to each other as much as possible. They communicate thoughtfulness, tenderness, and kindness. When couples experience this emotional orgasm, they want to prolong it as long as they can.

When both members of a couple experience romance simultaneously, it may be heavenly. A word of caution: When individuals are at different "mental places," when they travel at different speeds, or when they are just different in general, the feelings of romance may be accompanied by mutual frustration, or require significant understanding and patience. When one person feels strong romantic emotions and the other person does not, such qualities as understanding and patience may be limited and rational clarity may be obstructed. So, what happens when romance occurs simultaneously and at different speeds?

When It Comes, It Comes!

Unlike some aspects of a relationship, when a person experiences romantic feelings, those feelings seem to spontaneously burst forth. When two people are attracted to each other and have intense romantic feelings for each other, the relationship is propelled into a courtship high.

Couples in my study reported a steady increase in their romantic feelings from their initial meeting through their courtship. These feelings peaked at the time of the wedding ceremony. Although couples reported their intense romantic feelings decreasing somewhat throughout the marriage, romance was still rated as important.

In addition, throughout the relationship men rated their intense romantic feelings higher than women. What men and women, or different personality types, may understand intense romantic feelings to be can be quite different. Likewise, some people's life experiences may affect how deeply they can or will experience these feelings.

Some descriptions of intense romantic feelings were: "She was on my mind all the time"..."I couldn't wait until I saw him again"..."Strong emotion coupled with strong sexual desire"... "Passion"..."Giddy"..."Fascination"..."Desire to be together all the time"..."Strange and a little scary"..."A warm feeling"... "Dreamy"... "Being less selfish and *really wanting* to be kind and thoughtful"..."It's like being kissed and held close"..."Shared laughter at anything or nothing"..."Butterflies" and "Emotional, intimate love." For couples who have been married one time, the building and sustaining of intense romantic feelings seems to be important for relationship development.

Romance That Leads to Marriage

Romance is the emotion which often results in thoughtful behavior. When meeting with couples in premarital counseling sessions, I hear countless examples of loving gestures and romantic proposals. Many males seem to be on their best behavior at this time. *If they aren't, don't count on improvement after the wedding.*

Card shops, gift stores, florists, and long-distance services love people who are romantic, just as jewelry stores love men who are planning to pop the question. Some men must be at their creative, romantic best when they propose. While the wedding may be the bride's moment, the engagement can easily be the groom-to-be's moment.

I have heard hundreds of incredibly tender, heart-tuggingly romantic stories about proposals on a mountaintop at sunset. Or at home plate of a major league baseball park. Diamond engagement rings at the bottom of a Christmas stocking or in a serving of caviar. Proposals in the presence of 100 of their closest friends or 100 total strangers. Or privately in a college dorm room. If you are married, fondly remember that special time. If you are not married or engaged, plan something special. These are one-of-a-kind memories you can capture and savor forever.

Although some weddings take more detailed and intense planning than almost anything I can think of, the high and holy time of a couple's wedding is one of the most publicly romantic occasions we ever experience. In spite of obvious nervousness, most brides and grooms are filled with romantic love as they look at each other, repeat vows, and celebrate the beginning of their marriage.

For many people attending weddings, this is also a romantic time for them as they get caught up in the special nature of the event. They feel romantic because of their own loving relationship with a date or a mate. It's a fact that a number of couples who marry met at a wedding.

As a minister, I have a very privileged place. After having come to know a couple extremely well through our premarital sessions, I have a personal and professional investment in their lives and relationship. Then, to be in whispering distance as they share this most public intimate time in their lives, is indeed a privilege.

Standing there, I have seen scores of romantic and sometimes funny incidents unfold before my eyes. There was the time the bride forgot the groom's ring and I discreetly lent her my wedding ring. The time the wedding candles fell and as the bride, groom, and congregation gasped, I played fireman. When no one thought to pick up the from-out-of-town best man staying at a hotel several miles from the wedding site. And the infamous hot air balloon wedding where I sustained bruises because the initial landing attempt was quite rough. All of these happenings and many others are a part of the emotion which makes these wonderfully romantic events so powerful.

Waning Romance

If romance is not present within, and between, each person, this is a crucial issue.

I'll never forget the time a young woman I had been seeing in therapy because of incest brought her fiancé in for a session. She had indicated their relationship no longer had a romantic quality. I asked the young man why the romance had waned. He replied, "Oh, we're past that."

The young woman looked at her fiancé with an expression of shock and irritation.

"Being romantic is what you do to get a girl—and I have her now," he continued. "I'm too busy developing my business and making money to be romantic."

A lot of people may think this way. This young man was just frank and insensitive enough to say it.

As you might guess, this couple did not get married. He was unwilling to grow and she was equally unwilling to remain in a relationship without romance.

As a marriage ages, the intensity and frequency of romantic feelings may lessen. Even so, intense romantic feelings, which may have mellowed over the years, seem to remain important for the duration of the relationship.

The Poet and the Engineer

Sometimes people's personalities and backgrounds affect their expression of romantic feelings. That's the case with Judith and Bill. They were opposites who attracted each other when they met in their late 30s. Bill had never been married and Judith had divorced in her mid 20s. Each had led an adventuresome life before they met. After receiving her master's degree in British literature, Judith studied in England and traveled throughout Europe. Bill was a petroleum engineer and had spent several years working in the Middle East. A mutual acquaintance had introduced them. They hit it off immediately.

When Judith initially came to see me, they had been married about four years. She tearfully revealed she didn't think Bill loved her anymore. A literature teacher, she described herself as a hopeless romantic who loved Shakespeare and poetry.

Judith then confided that she told Bill every day how much she loved him. She said that he seemed to have great difficulty in uttering those same oh-so-important words to her.

Their courtship and the early part of their marriage had been frequently interrupted by Bill's international travel. He had recently taken a job which required minimal trips out of town. For the first time in their relationship, they were around each other *a lot*.

"We both waited a long time to get married," Judith sobbed. "We had such a romantic courtship. And now, for the past few months, our relationship has been empty."

After she had told me more about Bill, I realized he sounded like a man of action, not of words. I told her so. Then I suggested that she observe Bill to pinpoint if there were some things he did which might be his way of expressing love to her.

Bill came with Judith for the next session.

Describing himself as a good ol' boy from West Texas who had worked hard since childhood, Bill added that his mother and father had worked side by side on their ranch. "My mother dug just as many post holes as my dad." He said he never saw his parents hug or kiss. He said he never heard them say "I love you" to each other. And they never said "I love you" to any of their children.

"We just knew they loved us, but they were not expressive or demonstrative people," he explained. "I guess I'm like that too." He paused. "But I do love my wife."

I asked Judith if she had observed Bill doing things which might express love to her. "I think when Bill puts gas in my car, he's telling me he loves me. And when he washes my car, he's telling me he really loves me," she replied.

Almost in amazement, Bill blurted out, "Didn't you know that?"

Then came a telling revelation. "No, I didn't," Judith responded. "But I do now." "Still," she mused, "I'd love to hear those words from you. It would mean so much to me."

Judith asked Bill, "Honey, what could I do so that you feel loved?"

"You tell me all the time," Bill commented. "But, me, I like practical things. You know, things you do *for* me or things that save me time."

It was as natural as breathing for Judith to verbally and affectionately express her passionate and romantic feelings to Bill. But she seldom did those little non-verbal things which meant a lot to him. Judith committed herself to doing such things as making coffee for Bill in the mornings and picking up his clothes at the cleaners. Bill approvingly nodded and said, "Now you're talking my language."

Bill made a commitment to tell Judith several times a day that he loved her. He said that he would hug and kiss her more often. Judith volunteered to attend rodeos with Bill. Bill offered to accompany Judith to plays. They both vowed to have weekly dinner dates.

Bill did one more thing which really touched his wife. Each day, he wrote a "two-liner" and put it in her lunch box. His self-described "two-liners" were not great poetry, but they were wonderful love notes to Judith. I remember one that declared: "I love you more than I can say,/ but I love you more each day." And another that proclaimed: "I'm an engineer and you're a poet./ I love you so much and I want you to know it."

Both Bill and Judith were romantics, yet they expressed their love in completely different ways. After they carefully examined their own personalities and background differences and each other's genuine romantic expressions they once again shared romance. And they shared it in ways that were most meaningful to each of them.

Eternal Romantics

When I was a boy, we visited my mother's uncle several times a year. In the afternoons, we would sit on the front porch of Uncle Earl's comfortable home in the Northeast Texas community of Roxton. The house was on the main street of this little town of a few hundred people.

n a couple walked by holding hands or sat close to each other as they rode by in a passing car, Uncle Earl would chuckle and say, "Well, you can tell *they're* not married."

When couples are courting, this is a very romantic time in their lives. Couples often write, send cards, call, bring flowers, kiss longer, hug tighter, and steam up windows more at this time than at any other time in their relationship. No wonder people fall in love when a relationship has so much romance.

Romantic intensity and feelings are ever-changing. Sometimes the flames of romance are high. Sometimes the flames ebb. If you are in a relationship, keep fueling this fire. Keep "dating" each other. Keep being romantic.

A question I often ask couples is: "How long are your kisses?" I have no scientific evidence to support my hypothesis, but it is clear to me that a kiss which slides across a cheek on the way out the door does not warm many relationships. Long, passionate, romantic kisses are emissaries of romance—the emotional orgasm. Sharing that amazing pleasure with your mate, and sharing it often, will help create a relationship that will last a lifetime.

Romance Exercises

1. When you were growing up, how did your parents express romantic feelings toward each other?
2. How do you feel inside when you have intense romantic feelings?
3. If you are in a relationship, how do you feel when receiving intense romantic feelings from your partner?
4. If you are in a relationship, what helps your partner to experience intense romantic feelings?
5. What helps you to have intense romantic feelings?
6. What do you think will help your relationship to have intense romance for a lifetime?

Chapter 5
Commitment Means You Have to Work at It!

Several years ago I was speaking to an undergraduate Sociology of the Family class about marriage. I had just made the statement that I believed a couple had to *intentionally* work at a marriage for it to be good. An attractive young woman sitting on the front row raised her left hand, which was adorned with a diamond engagement ring about the size of her knuckle. She sighed breathlessly, "Well, if you have to work at it, it just must not be right." I thought, "How naive!"

Romantic feelings may occur effortlessly, but the commitment required to sustain an exclusive or a lifetime relationship requires significant effort from the couple. This chapter will address the all-important "C" word and what it really entails for the kind of marriage you want.

Commitment and Faithfulness—A Must

Not surprisingly, participants in my study rated commitment and fidelity as *the most important item* at the time of their marriage. It was the top-rated item for women during courtship and it was the second-rated item, behind physical attraction, for men during courtship. Men rated commitment and fidelity as the highest item of importance at the present time of their marriage and women rated it in the number two position (after emotional support, a matter which will be addressed in the next chapter).

Faithfulness

Although the focus of this chapter will be on commitment, which can imply faithfulness, let's briefly address this quality explicitly. Intimate, exclusive, engaged, and married couples must have trust in order to thrive and probably to survive. A key component to this trust is the faithfulness to the relationship. When a couple commits to faithfulness early in the relationship, during courtship, at the time of engagement, in the wedding service and during marriage, a person's word must be his or her bond. When this kind of commitment is made, it is not a license for complacency; it is an agreement which can free a relationship from anxiety and move the intimacy to an incredible new level.

Conversely, one of the most damaging events to a relationship is unfaithfulness on the part of one or both parties. Whether the unfaithfulness occurs before or during marriage, as a one-night stand or an ongoing affair, with a prostitute or as cybersex, the trust and even the sacredness of the relationship are damaged. Many guilty parties rationalize that they were not looking for an affair, it just happened. Or that they thought that no one would find out and no one would get hurt. This is really naive thinking. Of course there are times in our lives when we are stressed, vulnerable, or even tempted. Even so, there is no excuse for infidelity.

Unfaithfulness causes permanent damage. Some people and relationships heal after infidelities, but that healing process is usually very lengthy and not without memorable emotional scars.

In therapy, a contract which is often used with depressed persons is a "no suicide" contract. Essentially, patients make a commitment that they will not harm or kill themselves. This commitment they make to themselves in the presence of the therapist. Similarly, people can make a commitment to themselves that they will be faithful in a relationship. Whatever your relationship status, I encourage you to make a commitment to yourself that you will be faithful.

100 Percent Commitment

In a follow-up interview with one participating couple, they described the absolute necessity of commitment and fidelity to their relationship, an attitude shared by many couples. Laura said, "If I did not believe both of us were 100 percent committed and faithful to the relationship and would remain 100 percent faithful to each other, I would not have gotten married." Similarly, Jeff commented, "Because I had really come to know how committed Laura was to me and to our relationship, I totally trusted her. Also, I had been 100 percent faithful to Laura through our dating and engagement and I trusted myself. When we got married, we had that deep knowing that we would be faithful to each other for a lifetime."

I am not surprised by Laura and Jeff's use of "100 percent" in their description of commitment and fidelity. I use a 0 to 100 scale with couples in my office regarding their commitment to the relationship. For various reasons, some people are not committed to a relationship. They may have been initially committed, but the commitment level has waned. They may be scared of commitment. Or they may be unwilling to commit because they would rather remain uncommitted. Let's look at each of these challenges to commitment.

From Commitment to a Lack of Commitment

As a therapist, I find it an amazing and saddening experience to hear an individual or a couple who had been in a committed relationship express their strong negative feelings or lack of feelings regarding their mates. Often these are people who have been married for a number of years, who met and fell in love, courted and romanced each other, became engaged and got married, shared life's experiences as a couple, and bought a home and shared in the birthing and rearing of children. How can couples who were committed to each other and who traveled these years of marriage together no longer be committed to the relationship?

The answer to the above question is as unique as the uniqueness of each person and couple. Yet a common theme for couples whose marriages are lifeless or destructive is that one or both members of the union did not put forth the intentional, consistent effort necessary for the life and health of a viable marriage.

After a period of time, many persons focus less and less attention on their mates and focus more on other interests. A common example of this shift of attention is the person of either sex who focuses almost exclusively on work. The profession may be medicine, sales, engineering, construction, computers, entertainment, politics, management, teaching, coaching, ministry, or any other work. Plus, some parents focus so much attention on their children that the mate is neglected. Doing a good job at work and rearing children are both crucial events for economic security and childhood development. However, sometimes we really get out of balance.

One out-of-balance couple is Robert and Sharon. They met while they were in college, and after two years of marriage, their first child was born. Three years later their second child arrived. Robert and Sharon and their daughter and son made up an ideal family.

While Robert developed his career, Sharon focused her attention on child-rearing and volunteer work. In October of their 19th year of marriage, Robert had the opportunity to take a job in another city which offered him the possibility of tripling his salary. They already had a home in a prestigious neighborhood and all the trimmings, but Robert said the money was too good to turn down. Sharon really wanted to remain in their present home and way of life.

For the next seven months, Sharon stayed in their home, while their daughter completed her senior year of high school and their son completed junior high. Initially, Robert flew home almost every weekend. But by January, his trips home were infrequent and his job included more international travel. Robert and Sharon called each other less often.

When Sharon and the children moved in June to where Robert was employed, they moved into a huge house in that city's most exclusive area. From day one, Robert hardly ever had a pleasant thing to say to Sharon and spent very little time with his daughter and son. What had seemed an ideal family and a faithful and committed marriage was now a troubled and distant group of people.

Although the couple had always agreed that Sharon would remain a full-time mom until both children graduated from high school, Robert began urging Sharon to get a job. Without any discussions about being displeased with his marriage, Robert announced one evening to Sharon that he did not love her any more. He revealed that he had rented an apartment and was moving his things out that weekend.

What caused this once committed couple to come to this point? There are, of course, many factors to consider. A significant factor was that while living out of town away from his family, Robert focused less and less attention on his wife and children. He experienced the headiness of being in an exciting and powerful role with his new company. Also, he began to flirt with female employees and later had an affair with one of the women. This affair remained a secret until the divorce. Two months after the divorce was finalized, he and the much younger woman married.

The excitement of the new job and relationship in the absence of his usual way of life shifted Robert's priorities and commitments. The disruption of an intact family life and her hurt feelings about her husband's decision to leave the family to take the new job contributed to Sharon's lack of consistent effort to work even harder on the marriage. Robert had tripled his salary and they bought a huge home. Sharon focused her efforts into being both mom and dad to their children.

Neither Robert nor Sharon put forth a consistent, intentional commitment to their marital relationship during those months of transition. This type of effort is necessary in everyday living circumstances. Even more effort is necessary in those times in our relationships when there are extraordinary situations, such as moves and transfers, when a spouse returns to school or re-enters the workplace, when there are family illnesses or responsibilities, a job loss or a financial crisis, the birth of a child or an empty nest.

Marriage as a Concentration Camp

It's a major, life-changing decision to marry. Many people have concerns about entering or re-entering a committed relationship. Among the most common feelings which result in hesitancy to commit to a relationship is fear. Whenever people tell me their fears, I often capitalize them because I know FEARS can be so powerful.

An example of fear of commitment is the case of Dave. He was in a two-year relationship with a beautiful young woman who adored him. But he was really scared of committing to marry his girlfriend.

One day I asked Dave what his image of marriage was. After thoughtfully considering my question, he said, "My image of marriage is a concentration camp with couples in a drab atmosphere walking slowly with somber expressions on their faces." I responded, "No wonder you don't want to get married!" Dave went on to say that he had developed this image because his parents had a lifeless marriage, one in which they just existed with each other. He added that many of his friends and professional associates had bad marriages, cheated on their wives, or were divorced. No wonder Dave said he was about 40 percent committed to this relationship.

After addressing this horrible image of marriage and its origins, Dave began to look at his girlfriend, himself, and their relationship through clearer eyes. This enabled Dave and his girlfriend to more freely address their relationship. They became engaged, got married, and to this day are very committed to each other.

If part of you really wants to have a good marriage, but another part of you does not, examine that negative part, that fear or insecurity. How did you develop your fear of commitment? Did experiences from your parents' lifeless or destructive marriage contribute to your fear? Are you are still carrying scars from your parents' divorce? Are you still emotionally wounded from a previous intimate relationship? Having addressed these issues, you can then more adequately focus on your present relationship with a clearer mind.

I'm Not Going to Commit

Although most people marry, some do not. This is a choice each of us has. A number of couples experience the difficult situation that arises when one person wants a committed relationship or marriage and the other does not. Every year I see couples who are in this boat.

Kenny is a young professional athlete who's consistently been a winner in sports and in life. When he and his girlfriend came in for a session, he was distraught that she would not commit to marrying him. She explained that she was only 23 and had no intentions of marrying *anyone* at this time in her life.

She had not had a bad childhood. In fact, she had a good relationship with her parents. She indicated that her life goals included being a world traveler and working in different cultures around the globe.

Kenny had fallen in love with this attractive, adventurous young woman and tried his best to change her mind. He said that his philosophy was that if you just work at something hard enough, you'll get it. While this philosophy has much merit, Donna was not an "it" which he could get.

Their 18-month relationship had been great until Kenny began asking Donna about their getting married. When she told him she really enjoyed their relationship and thought he was a great guy, but that she did not want to get married, Kenny was shocked, hurt, disappointed, and frustrated.

Finally, Kenny began to accept that he could not change her mind. This was a painful grief experience. He realized, however, that it was crucial for him to get on with his life rather than continue to put himself through torture. If you've ever been in Kenny's or Donna's shoes, you know how difficult these relationships can be. BOTH people must be willing to make a commitment, or the relationship will not work or progress.

The Commitment to Marriage, But…

Couples enter a second level of commitment when they are committed to BEING married. There is nothing necessarily wrong with this type of relationship, but it is often a complacent or "survival" marriage. These are couples who stay together for the kids' sake, for societal reasons, religious reasons, or financial reasons. If this is satisfactory for you, hang in there. Sad to say, but probably true, many couples remain in a survival relationship and never experience a thriving marriage.

If you are in this kind of marriage, I have a couple of suggestions. One, find a good time to talk with your mate and ask him or her if there are some things YOU can do that might make the relationship better. Or you might give your mate a card or a letter in which you write that you want to be a better mate and that you would appreciate some suggestions on the enclosed sheet of paper to be returned in the enclosed envelope. This may sound somewhat indirect. But remember that some people respond better on the spot, while others need a little time to think about a topic. Also, some people respond better to spoken ideas, while others appreciate the written word.

You might try one of these suggestions or come up with a method you think would work in your situation. Next, follow through by intentionally doing the things your mate requested or by discussing them and doing them. Ideally, your mate will take the hint and ask you for the same information.

If your mate is not very responsive to moving beyond a "being" relationship, you may, like numerous other people, find other means of fulfillment. Many people I have known over the years who have less than fulfilling marriages have found fulfillment in their work, volunteering, hobbies, friends, children and grandchildren, physical activities, and spiritual growth.

One such person was Martha. She was in her mid-40s and very active, but her husband, Ed, was in his late 50s and in poor health. It was the second marriage for each and he had helped to rear her two children. As his health declined, Ed became more and more difficult to live with. He frequently yelled at Martha and demanded her attention. Or he told her to get out of his life and to just hire a good cook and maid to take care of him. Martha's dilemma was: "Should I put up with his treatment of me or should I leave him?"

She thoroughly explored her feelings and options. Finally, she decided there was a third choice. For her, it meant beginning a new career, playing bridge again, and getting re-involved in her church. She remained married to her husband and did the best she could to brighten his day when she was home. She commented that the marriage was not great, but she handled it the best she could and made a good life for herself.

I'm Very Committed

A third kind of commitment is that of a person who can honestly say that he or she is very committed to the relationship. One man who has been married for 11 years said he was faithful to his wife and committed to her. But he added that if he evaluated how lovingly he treated her, he would have to give himself a score of 30. He revealed that he spent so much time at his job and working on his MBA degree that he ignored his wife and children. He looked at his wife and confessed, "I've not taken you out on a date in over two years."

Since relationships are dynamic, most of us could not honestly say we are 100 percent committed to our mate all of the time. Many people I see in therapy are very successful professionally. Most of us know that it takes much effort and consistent commitment to succeed in our work or in other areas of our lives. I sometimes ask a person, "If you treated your job the way you treat your marriage, what would happen?" Many times they will respond by saying, "I'd be put on probation or fired!"

The same thing happens in relationships—we can be put on relationship probation or fired. Still, others may say, "But I get paid at my job and I have to have an income." While this may be a true statement, in order to have a lifetime marriage, commitment to another person and a meaningful relationship can be the most fulfilling experience of our lives. Bankruptcy in relationships is usually the result of couples withdrawing too much from their mates and/or failing to make adequate deposits into the marriage account.

An example of a bankrupt marriage is that of George and Leslie. When they sat on opposite ends of the long sofa in my office with George's body facing the door and Leslie's body facing the window at the other side of my office, it did not take a psychological genius to diagnose the state of their relationship.

Leslie complained that George did not give any attention to her or to their two young children. With her eyes flashing angrily and her arms crossed, she described the following daily routine. Upon arriving home from work, George would still be talking on his cellular phone as he came in the door, would walk past her and the children, and go to his study still talking on the phone. She was really disgusted with George and indicated she thought their marriage had died.

Drawing on my days as a hospital chaplain, I asked, "If your marriage were a patient in the hospital, where would it be?" Leslie said she thought it would be in the intensive care unit on life support—the support she was giving it. George rationalized that it was not that bad, but later he agreed that their marriage might be in intensive care, with Leslie giving it IVs while he was absent.

George is a very successful attorney and I asked him what helped him to be so successful. He said that when he entered the courtroom, he knew he had worked harder on the case than anyone else. That made him better prepared than the opposing attorneys.

I complimented him for being so successful as an attorney, for working so hard on his cases, and for being the best-prepared attorney in a case. Then I asked him how hard he had been working on his marriage and how he prepared to greet his wife and children when he entered their home. He winced and confessed, "You got me...not well at all."

George suddenly came to a poignant realization: that he had been so caught up in becoming successful the past couple of years that he had neglected his family, especially his wife.

At our next session, the body language of George and Leslie was quite different. They sat closer to each other, were turned toward each other, and had pleasant facial expressions. Leslie smilingly said, "He's been doing a lot better."

George related that when he closed the door at his office, he began to think positive and loving thoughts about his wife and children. During his 20- to 25-minute drive home, he thanked God for his wife and children and prayed for God to help him be a focused and loving husband and dad. George said he was intentionally working on these most precious relationships and that when he entered his home it was as a good husband and dad.

Commitment Means Effort

To be 100 percent committed to a relationship means that every day you'll try your very best to be the very best husband or wife you can be. This does not imply perfection, whatever that is; but it does mean that you must put forth real effort.

It also means being committed to understanding your mate as best you can. I do not believe we are humanly capable of *totally* understanding another person. But I do believe that to have good, growing, fulfilling relationships, we must become students of our mates so we can understand them better and better.

Remember the Poet and Engineer from the previous chapter? The Poet began doing those little practical things—bringing him coffee and picking up his clothes from the cleaners—that meant a lot to her husband. And the Engineer began telling his wife several times a day that he loved her and writing "two-liners" to express his affection. They are a good example of a couple who intentionally thought about what would be loving expressions to each other.

Too often we only think about what "I" would want. An example I often share with couples is the stereotypical story of the man who wants a shotgun more than anything else for Christmas and the woman who wants diamond earrings for her gift. Christmas comes and he gives her a shotgun and she gives him diamond earrings. That's a silly story, but it illustrates what couples often experience. We give to the other person what we would want. The more loving thought would be: "Knowing my mate the way I do, this is what he/she would really appreciate."

Commitment means not being selfish, self-absorbed, or complacent; commitment means clearly, intentionally, and lovingly considering what would be important to your mate and following through on it.

Commitment Exercise

1. On a 1 to 100 scale, how committed are you to the relationship in thought, word, deed? Be honest. Translate these numbers into descriptions of your commitment.
2. What will you do so you will never be unfaithful to your mate?
3. Will you commit to be faithful in your relationship? If so, say it out loud and write it, including your signature and date. Feel good about making this commitment.

4. What will you do on a consistent basis to keep your relationship growing?
5. What are some extraordinary situations you are facing or will face which could be stressful on your relationship?
6. What will you do in these times of greater stress or crisis to keep your relationship thriving?
7. What are some of your fears about commitment?
8. What are you willing to do to address these fears?
9. Are there other fears you have about your relationship? If so, discuss them.
10. Are you in a relationship in which only one of you is committed? If so, will you address this issue with your partner?
11. Are you in a complacent or survival relationship? If so, ask and write to your mate about what you could do to make the relationship better.
12. In addition to your relationship, what are other areas of your life which are fulfilling? Or, what will you do to add more fulfillment to your life?
13. How are you intentionally and consistently putting forth effort toward a thriving relationship?
14. How can you MORE intentionally and consistently put forth MORE effort toward a thriving relationship?
15. Clearly, intentionally, and lovingly think of your mate and what you can do that he or she would really appreciate. Then DO IT!

PART FOUR:
THE KEYS TO A THRIVING MARRIAGE

Chapter 6
What Women Want More Than Anything Else And Men Crave Too

As you read this chapter, you may note that the headings refer to gender differences. Although stereotypical gender difference is not the most important issue in marriage, there are some heart-felt qualities which most women and most men indicate are vital for a fulfilling relationship. However, both *emotional support* for women and *encouragement* for men refer to the same part of us humans—our feelings!

In a relationship, especially in an intimate relationship, we want to feel loved. We want to feel special. We want to feel important to our mates. We want to feel understood. We want to feel supported. Along with commitment and fidelity, emotional support and encouragement can make the difference in relationships being intimate, thriving, and lifelong.

What Women Really Want

When I was on staff at First United Methodist Church in Richardson, Texas, I was working *a lot* of hours per week. I'm not bragging or complaining, just stating a fact. During that time, our daughter Laura and son Adam were preschool ages, so Kathleen carried a majority of the responsibility for rearing them.

I was shocked when Kathleen was totally ho-hum when I excitedly announced to her that I was going to take a group from our church to Israel. All I could imagine was the fantastic opportunity to see where Abraham journeyed, Moses viewed the promised land, David ruled, Jesus was born and lived, and several major religions developed. What I did not imagine was that Kathleen needed me and the emotional support I could supply at this extremely important time in our lives.

Emotional Support

Whether it is during courtship, engagement, early marriage, when the children are little, during the middle years, or after retirement, women really want emotional support from the men in their lives.

Results from my study indicate that *emotional support is what women want more than anything else from men*. This quality was paramount from their first meeting. It increased in importance through each stage of the relationship, and reached its greatest significance at the present time of their marriage. Whether they had been married two months or 56 years, women wanted emotional support from their spouse first and foremost.

For Men Only

We men may know IT—emotional support. We may have heard or read about IT many times. Our girlfriends, fiancées, and wives have probably told us this important information over and over. However, we often fail to respond well. If we want to have a great lifetime, thriving marriage, we must intentionally and consistently give emotional support to our mates.

What Can I Do Now? I Hope It Is Not Too Late!

One day I received three phone calls from a man. We played telephone tag for a few hours before we had our conversation. He said that he was having "some family problems."

This could have meant almost anything, but he clarified his statement by saying he and his wife were having "marital problems."

Next he proclaimed that he was a great provider. He and his wife had a beautiful home. They had two great children, ages 6 and 2, and he was very good with them. He paused for a few moments before painfully confessing that he had never met his wife's emotional needs during their eight-year marriage. I could sense the terrible anguish inside this man as he told me that his wife said she was numb in her feelings for him. She had given up trying to get emotional support from him, adding that the only reason she had stayed with him this long was because of their children.

Then, in an alarmed tone, he said she was spending more and more time with a couple of her women friends. One was divorced. The other was going through a divorce.

The man cleared his throat. A few seconds crept by. In a dejected voice, he explained that his wife had told him she had talked with an attorney. Before concluding his story, he tacked on, almost convincingly, that he would understand if his wife had turned to another man for emotional support.

"What can I do?" he cried. He said he had started bringing her flowers every day. He tried to hug and kiss her. He was now telling her how much he loved her, how beautiful she was, that he would do *anything* she wanted. He lamented that she yelled at him, booming, "Why haven't you done any of this in the last several years? I don't want anything from you now!"

I sincerely hope you never have an experience like this. I hope you never have to feel these painful, scary, desperate feelings about your relationship because of how you have treated or not treated your mate. I hope you never treat your mate as this man did his.

Most of us men have a lot to learn about relationships, especially intimate ones. Earlier I stated that we need to be students of our mates. They will teach us a lot if we will pay attention. In fact, the information in this section comes from women in my study. They are the experts.

Check With Those Who Know

If we want expert information on business matters, we consult with a business expert. If we want expert information on investments, we consult with an investment expert. If we want expert information on golf, tennis, fishing, hunting, football, baseball, basketball, hockey, bowling, sailing, hang gliding, or spitting and scratching, we watch sports channels, listen to sports radio, read the sports pages and magazines, and consult with other sports experts.

If we want expert information on our relationship, we need to consult with our mates. But first, read a few more pages so that you will grasp the importance of this venture—and make a commitment to follow through on your part. If you implement this information, there is a strong likelihood you will have a mate with whom you can share a lifelong, thriving relationship.

Undivided Attention

One of the greatest gifts we can ever give to our mates is our unwavering, undivided attention. That does not mean listening while we have channel changers in our hands or newspapers, magazines, or books in front of our faces. No leftover thoughts from work. No eyes glancing at the sports scores trailing across the bottom of the television screen or staring at the ceiling.

Most of us guys can do only one thing at a time anyway. So,

if our mates are communicating with us, it is important to give our full attention to them. Look at her. But don't stare resentfully or impatiently. Let the rest of the sights, sounds, and thoughts of the jungle fade away. Then look at, listen to and think about your mate.

When we are giving our mates our undivided attention, we are expressing emotional support. Our mates can usually tell when we are really with them or only partly there. Undivided attention is a quiet gift. But it speaks volumes when we care enough to really be present with them.

Listen to What Is Being Said

There's more. Pay attention to what is being said: the content. Each sentence is important. Each paragraph is important. But often our listening attention span and the amount our mates need to share are not equal.

A young engineering student and his theater major girlfriend had a problem in this area. When his girlfriend paused while sharing the events of her day, he would butt in to tell her about *his* day. She informed him that her pause was only for dramatic emphasis on what she was saying.

After some coaching in communication skills, they agreed that when she had finished what she was saying she would let him know by saying, "Thank you for listening." Until then, he would continue to listen.

Much has been written about men jumping in to fix problems or give advice. Sometimes the comment is made, "You only want me to listen?" The word "only" sounds as if listening is so simple, meager, or insignificant. Not so! *Listening well is one of the most important qualities for a good relationship*. Really listening to what is being said communicates that you care enough to give your mate your *full* attention.

Listen Actively

Active listening is a term often used to describe good listening. As listeners, we communicate too. Have you ever heard someone ask, "Are you listening? Because I could not tell whether you were or you weren't."

A cousin of mine, Virginia, is a former high school French teacher. Quite a talker, she told this story about Bob, her late husband. *He* knew how to actively listen.

While Virginia was talking with a group of friends at a French Club gathering, a French woman engaged Bob in conversation. Eventually, Virginia told the woman in French that Bob could not speak her language. The French woman protested, declaring she was sure Bob was very conversant in French. Virginia was quite puzzled by this comment.

After the French Club meeting, she asked Bob what had gone on. He just shrugged and explained that when the French woman was talking and nodding her head up and down, he also nodded his head up and down and said, "Oui, oui." Likewise, when the woman was speaking and shook her head from side to side, he also shook his head from side to side and exclaimed, "Non, non."

I'm not suggesting that you practice this with your mate. It is, however, a good idea to occasionally nod your head. This communicates "I care about what you are saying...I care about you."

Another aspect of active listening is occasionally checking to see if you are on track with the content of what your mate is expressing. For example, reiterate or clarify what is being said. During one of our sessions, the theater student was telling her engineering student boyfriend about wanting to visit her parents during their spring break from school. He said, "So, you're saying that you would prefer to leave Saturday morning rather than Friday afternoon. Am I understanding you correctly?"

When he clarified the information, she beamed and said warmly, "Yes, that's right."

Then she related how different this was because he had hardly ever clarified information with her. Instead, he usually was quiet. She assumed he understood and he assumed he understood. However, in the past they both had often assumed incorrectly and major arguments erupted about schedules, timing, and plans. During the session with me, both were clear about their plans and had positive feelings about each other.

Listen to Feelings

Of course, emotional support is about feelings. It is just as important to listen to your mate's feelings as to the content. Listening to feelings is similar to listening to the music in a song. Music conveys the mood and the emotions of what is being expressed. Listening conveys, "I care about your feelings...I *really* care about you."

People who are not very aware of their feelings are often confused when someone asks them what their feelings are. Men in therapy sessions will often say they have no idea what their mates are feeling. I will ask them if they think their mates are happy or upset. Usually, men will respond by saying something like, "Well, I sure know she's not happy or we wouldn't be here." If that's the gist of their comment, I say, "Great! You have an idea that your mate is upset, so let's start there."

This starting point is similar to not being able to identify an oboe in an orchestra. We may know that the oboe is in the woodwind section or at least which side of the stage the sound is coming from. If we have an idea of the direction from whence our mate's feelings are coming, we can respond to them. For example, if her feelings are not coming from the happy side, a good rule of thumb is to say something like, "Are you upset about something, honey?" If she says, "Yes," be glad that you are on the correct side of the orchestra.

When their mates are upset, men generally get defensive, confused or scared. It may be their guilty consciences kicking in or it may be a lack of training. If your mate says she is upset, be courageous and make an invitation—"Tell me your feelings." If you invite her to share her feelings and *listen well* while you give her your *undivided attention*, you are giving her what she genuinely and deeply wants—emotional support. You care about her feelings. This is the heart of the matter. This is intimacy.

There are some of you who are able to—with unerring accuracy—read your mate's specific feelings. If you are, my congratulations to you. Most of us have one "general purpose" radar dish that can pick up only enemy or friendly. Even if we only use general words like "upset" or "happy" in response to our spouses' expressions of feelings, women will tell us more specifically what they are feeling.

For example, the young engineering student expressed to his theater major girlfriend that she seemed "upset" when he was late returning from the library one night. She clarified the situation by saying that she was "really worried" that something might have happened to him. He was relieved by her clarification because he thought her upset feelings probably meant she was mad at him.

Still another suggestion about understanding how your mate feels is to ask for her help. Say to your mate, "Help me to understand how you feel." This is better than asking for directions when you're lost. Most women know we guys need some help in the feelings department. So, when we communicate that we want to understand how they feel, we are in the ballpark of emotional support. We may never completely understand how our mates feel, but if we communicate that we will appreciate their helping us to understand, we are on the same team and team spirit is being built.

Some of the information here may seem rather simplistic. Be assured, however, that no matter how in tune or sophisticated you may be, these essentials of undivided attention and listening to and responding to their content and feelings make a profound and positive difference in relationships.

More About Feelings

There is a real likelihood that your mate has more feelings than just happy and upset. What do you do then? An exercise I have found to be most helpful to couples is for them to make a list of their various moods and feelings and then to tell their mates what they want from them at that time or how they hope their mates would respond.

When angry, for example, some people want to be held. Others want to be left alone. When worried, some people want to be reassured while others want to think things out loud. During hormonal mood swings, some women want to make love while others don't want to be touched. At the end of this chapter you will have the opportunity to complete an exercise in which you and your mate can share information with each other that may be extremely helpful in times of anger, frustration, confusion, sadness, disappointment, depression, fear, stress, sickness, accomplishment, or joy.

Even if you have been in a relationship for some time, it does not mean you are a mind reader or know all the right stuff to do when your mate has particular feelings. Therefore, having some guidelines, skills or responses in mind greatly improves your ability to respond appropriately to your mate when feelings are more sensitive and relationships are more easily affected.

To hone this much-needed skill, become more sensitive to phrases, sighs, tears, and smiles. Ask your mate to help you know what she means and what she wants when she says: "Do you still love me?" or "I need some alone time." or "I'm too tired." Ask her to tell you want it means when she displays particular facial expressions or body language. We guys are often better at picking up the nuances of a baseball pitcher, a hunting dog, or our boss's moods than we are of picking up the facial and body expressions of our mates. Most of us have at least some room for growth in this area. So, ask the expert—your mate.

The Power of "I Love You"

Most women like to hear their mates tell them they love them. Some women report that the only time their husbands say that they love them is when they want to have sex. We'll discuss sex in a later chapter. But for now, guys, let's focus on saying "I love you."

Some women want to be told several times a day that they are loved. Some men say they just don't do that kind of thing. These men state they will only tell their mates when they really mean it—maybe once or twice a week. What we have here is more than an inability to put three words together.

If the man is willing to work on this issue the way the good ol' boy from West Texas who was married to the literature teacher did, progress can be made. If you have a difficulty saying these words to your mate, ask yourself why you are unwilling to do this. Is it because you didn't grow up saying those words? Is it because you really do not love her? Is it because you think you have to feel deep, deep passion before you can say these words? Is it because you are not that committed to the relationship? Is it because you feel vulnerable or trapped if you say these words? Is it because you are stubborn and won't do it because she wants you to verbalize your love?

If it is troublesome for you to say those three wonderful words, I encourage you to examine yourself carefully and discuss this with your mate, a friend, or a therapist. *Difficulty in verbalizing your love will undoubtedly become a major problem in your relationship.*

On the other hand, some of you have little difficulty verbalizing your love. Good for you!

- Tell her in the morning and evening
- Tell her softly and strongly
- Tell her tenderly and passionately
- Tell her on special occasions and out of the clear blue
- Tell her while listening to music or watching a ball game
- Tell her looking into her eyes
- Tell her whispering into her ear
- Tell her on the phone
- Tell her in writing
- Tell her at that special restaurant
- Tell her while eating leftovers
- Tell her when she feels on top of the world
- Tell her when she feels like her world has collapsed
- Tell her while you're working in the yard together
- Tell her at weddings
- Tell her while you're walking
- Tell her while you're waiting in a line
- Tell her on the airplane
- Tell her while you're in a traffic jam
- Tell her in the bathroom
- Tell her on the front porch
- Tell her!

Show Her

Another aspect of emotional support women like and need is thoughtfulness. For most people, verbalized love means a lot more when it is also expressed in actions. "Talk is cheap... watch their feet" is one of my favorite sayings. So is the well-worn but true maxim: "Actions speak louder than words."

Expressions of love may include taking on some household responsibility such as vacuuming and cleaning. Many guys seem to do things when asked, but they may not take the initiative. Check with your mate if there are some things you can do around the house or if assuming more responsibility would help her to feel more emotionally supported.

Often I speak to groups of young mothers such as Early Childhood PTAs, community and church mothering groups, and Mothers of Multiples. From them I have learned a number of do's and don'ts:

**Do be an involved dad who will feed children, bathe them, and change their diapers.*

**When arriving home from work, take responsibility for the child or children for a while.*

**Take care of your child or children so she can take a leisurely bath or even go to the bathroom without being interrupted.*

**Pitch in regularly without having to be asked.*

**Don't ask sarcastically, "What have you been doing all day while I've been working?"*

**Don't say, "When I take care of the kids, I don't have any problems with them."*

**Don't ask, "Why are you so tired?"*

Whether you have children or not, there are a number of do's and don'ts which your mate will experience as emotional support.

**Hug her more and grab her less.*

**Clean the bathroom.*
**Bring her flowers.*
**Be more supportive and less critical of her work.*
**Support her educational pursuits or volunteer activities.*
**Compliment her appearance and beauty.*
**Read a relationship book with her.*

Emotional support is a big deal. Check with the expert about what she wants. Hear it. Do it. You will greatly benefit and so will your mate. Men, let's thrive in our relationships!

What Men Really Want

When I asked a group of married couples about what they thought men want as emotional support or encouragement, one woman quickly and candidly responded, "The consistent, considerate opposite of nagging." We all laughed, but I think she has her finger on the pulse point of many men.

Similar to women, men rated their emotional needs being met by their mate as increasingly important in their relationship. By the time men had been married anywhere from two months to 56 years, they rated only commitment and fidelity from their spouses as slightly more important than emotional support. Their emotional needs, however, were frequently described as encouragement. In this chapter, we will analyze and flesh out what may be absolutely the most important ingredient in a fulfilling, lifetime marriage.

For Women Only

Not surprisingly, women in my study consistently rated their marital relationship as being more important than men did, although men in the study increasingly rated relationship items as more important as the relationship developed. Furthermore, emotional support from their spouses was only slightly more important for women than for men. One thing is clear—men have emotional needs too.

Recognize Their Hard Work

For most men, their jobs, careers, or professions are more than just economic means. *A man's identity is often synonymous with his work.* When you complain about your mate's long hours at work, not leaving the job at the workplace, or not wanting to talk about his job, he will often react defensively. Men are often very territorial about this intricate part of themselves. Complaining about their jobs is similar to complaining about their inner core of being or criticizing their favorite sports franchise. Face it, they often are hypersensitive about the subject.

So What Is a Woman to Do?

Men tell me they really like it when their mates commend them for their hard work and even brag on them. One man said that his wife really encourages him in his hobby of softball. "She tells me how proud she is of me for working out, practicing, and giving it all I have in a game. I just love it when she tells me those things. It may be my male ego or whatever, but it feels great. So, one day I told her I wished she would encourage me and brag on me regarding my job the way she does about softball. And you know what? She told me that was a good suggestion."

That man went on to say that when his wife is encouraging about his work, he has a lot better attitude toward her and wants to come home rather than avoid her possible nagging. This may not work with all men. *But most men seem to thrive on their mates being proud of them for working hard...not just for the money, but for their effort.*

Encourage Their Interests

If your mate has an interest or hobby, he will probably appreciate your encouragement or positive comments regarding this passion. This statement may seem strange and may make you wonder: "If I want him to spend more time with me, why would I encourage a hobby that keeps him away from me?" Let's look at this situation.

When Phyllis came to therapy, she was very distressed about her "lifeless marriage." She described her husband as very successful professionally and handsome but distant. Phyllis, a former professional singer, described herself as being very passionate—and critical. She explained the thing she resented the most was her husband's regular attendance at numerous auto races around the country, in addition to his heavy business travel.

One week Troy had a business trip to North Carolina. There just happened to be a NASCAR race scheduled that weekend in the area of his meeting. Phyllis reported to me that she was furious because he seemed to want to attend the race a lot more than he wanted to return home to be with her and their children.

Every time Troy wanted to go to a race, Phyllis gave him a blistering piece of her mind about being so selfish and immature and not caring about her and the kids. I asked her if this improved the marriage. "Not at all," she responded. "But maybe some day he will get the message and become more of a family man."

Sometimes we believe if we just keep hammering away at someone the light bulb will flash and magically our mates will become what we want them to be. Since Phyllis admitted her consistent, critical nagging was not working, I asked her, "What would it be like if you said to your husband that you hoped he had a good business trip to North Carolina *and* that you truly hoped he'd enjoy himself at the race?"

Phyllis sat in stunned silence for a few moments because I had suggested an idea opposite to what she had in mind and had consistently demonstrated. The color eventually returned to her face and her wide eyes relaxed a little. Then she admitted, "Well, that would certainly be different."

Although Phyllis really did want Troy to want to be home for the weekend, she confessed that her negative, guilt-tripping approach only resulted in her husband's distancing himself from her. Initially she said she'd be lying if she told him she hoped he'd have a good time at the race. But after exploring her feelings of frustration and resentment about the issue, Phyllis ultimately decided she had nothing to lose if she expressed good wishes to her husband. She came to realize that instead of their parting exploding into another painful fight, it could possibly be a positive step in the right direction for a better relationship.

A couple of days later I received a phone call from Phyllis. She reported that when she had told Troy she hoped he had a good time at the race his jaw dropped in amazement. After he had asked her with sincerity several times if she was feeling well, Phyllis told him she wanted to be his friend and not his enemy...that she wanted him to know she really did care for him. Before he left, Troy, still somewhat in shock, said that he'd like to take her out to dinner the next weekend. Even though Phyllis and Troy had several issues to resolve, this expression of encouragement was an important step in breaking their cycle of resentment.

What are your mate's interests? Watching sports on television? Playing golf or softball with his buddies? Going to baseball, football, basketball, or hockey games? Playing tennis, rugby, or cards? Going to horse or auto races? Woodworking, bicycling, or reading? Fishing, hunting, or hiking? Participating in civic, service, or religious organizations or a lodge? Music, art, or theater? Computers, gardening, or the stock market? Cars, horses, or cattle? Flying, sailing, or boating? If it is not illegal or immoral, would you be willing to be more encouraging to your mate regarding his interests? Would he like for you to share with him in any of these interests or would he prefer for these to be his own interests?

To Be Left Alone or Embraced

Some men really like being left alone. Gene was a salesman who was quite introverted. He joked that he had met his "people quota" by noon each work day. Because of this, when he came home, the last thing on his mind was people contact. But his extroverted, passionate wife greeted him with hugs and kisses and their two young children jumped on him when he returned home from work. She could not understand why he would not want this type of greeting—she would.

When they came to therapy, he felt engulfed and smothered by his wife. She felt unloved and rejected by her husband.

After a session or two, they agreed that Gene would benefit from about 30 minutes of alone time when he arrived home. Gene said that vegging in front of the television in their bedroom would help him to unwind so that he could more warmly greet his wife and children. If you or your mate need some alone unwinding time, discuss this matter so that your together time will be more enjoyable.

Some men really want a lot of attention. Walt is a regional manager for a computer company. His job requires him to travel away from home about one week per month. Both he and Edie, a corporate attorney, had been married before. They were very committed to making this one work. Walt's primary concern was that Edie was so self-sufficient and work-oriented that she did not give him much attention. Edie commented she was not a "high maintenance" woman and did not require much affection and attention. They revealed they enjoyed their successful careers, bicycling, and their involvement in the volunteer house-building organization Habitat for Humanity.

Walt and Edie came to me for a marital checkup. They had been married for two years and described their marriage as good. But at Walt's suggestion, they made an appointment to evaluate their marriage and to make it better. He said he had mentioned to Edie that he wanted more attention and she had responded by saying she thought they did a lot of things together. In clarifying his concerns further, Walt stated more specifically he would appreciate such things as Edie's initiating hugs, kisses, sitting in his lap, and being more playful with him. Edie was very agreeable to his suggestions. She even decided, without telling Walt, that she would slip thoughtful, funny or sexy cards or notes into his suitcase, briefcase, or coat pocket. In a followup session a couple of months later, Walt was especially happy about these little surprises Edie gave him while he was traveling.

What kinds of attention would your mate like? (We'll get to sex in a later chapter.) Here are some attention-getting suggestions I've heard from my sessions with couples:

**Leaving a love note on his car seat*
**Taking him out to lunch*
**Preparing a candlelight dinner at home*
**Giving him a massage*
**Washing his hair*
**Tidying up the house*
**Telling him you really think he is a good man who's bright, handsome, or funny*

**Telling him you appreciate him*
**Calling him at work simply to tell him you love him*
**Leaving a loving E-mail or voicemail message*
**Playing footsie with him under the table*
**Kissing him passionately in an elevator (Empty or not. It's your call.)*
**Buying him the kind of underwear he really likes*

Your Relationship's Heart

Emotional support and encouragement are really the heart of every couple's relationship. No matter how self-sufficient, independent, introverted, extroverted, youthful, or old a woman or man may be, we all have feelings—and crave the positive feelings we derive from emotional support and encouragement. These warm, fuzzy feelings are very important gifts we can give our mate. And those gifts nurture intimate, thriving relationships.

Exercise for Emotional Support and Encouragement

(Men, write responses to these items and refer to them often.)

1. Why do YOU think emotional support is so important for your mate?
2. What do YOU think your mate wants from you regarding emotional support?
3. Ask HER what she really wants from you that is emotionally supportive.
4. While listening to your mate, be very patient and listen closely for both content and feelings.
5. Ask your mate to tell you her various feelings and moods. Then, ask her how she would appreciate you responding to her at these times.

6. Ask your mate about clues or cues you might be more sensitive to and respond to.
7. Check with your mate if she would like for you to tell her more often that you love her. If so, lovingly tell her more often—and enjoy doing it!
8. Check with your mate about what you can do that would help her to feel more emotionally supported. (Regarding work, relationships, etc.)

Listen well. Follow through. Feel good about doing these loving items.

(Women, write responses to these items and refer to them often.)

1. How would your mate like for you to be supportive to him regarding his work? If you're not sure, ask him.
2. What are your mate's interests and hobbies?
3. How could you be more encouraging to him regarding his interests?
4. Would your mate like for you to share with him in any of these interests or would he prefer for them to be his own interests?
5. Does your mate want more alone time? If so, discuss this with him.
6. Does your mate want more attention? If so, discuss this with him.
7. What kind of special attention would your mate like?
8. What helps your mate to feel really special and loved?

Chapter 7
These Things Are Important to Me. Are They Important to You? Interests, Values, and Beliefs

Interests and Hobbies

When I met my wife Kathleen, I thought she was wonderful, beautiful, and fantastic. When I discovered she also liked baseball—wow!—I realized she was even more remarkable than I had previously thought.

Beginning in the second grade, I developed a passion for baseball as a player and a fan. As a child growing up in the farming and ranching community of Belk, Texas, I dreamed about the Dodgers. Meanwhile, Kathleen grew up in Chicago and Tulsa, Oklahoma, attending baseball games and learning how to score a game as soon as she could print. Granted, our relationship would probably have progressed well without this particular ingredient, but our shared love for the game added a special spark. By the way, we still love going to our beloved Texas Rangers games.

In this chapter we will explore the importance of interests, hobbies, values, and beliefs in a relationship. When romance is aflame, different beliefs, values, or interests may blur or even seem unimportant. As couples *really* get to know each other, however, it becomes increasingly important to discuss these items. In their initial meetings, couples may seek to establish some sense of commonality on a relatively elementary level.

In their first meeting, Fritz told Susan he had graduated from the University of Wisconsin. Susan responded that she had graduated from the University of Texas, but her cousin was a student at the Wisconsin university. Before their first date was over, they knew they both liked to watch football games, wanted to play more golf, and enjoyed eating Mexican food. This initial level of discussing interests is only a beginning stage of knowing each other's interests.

Discussing Interests

I see several adolescents in therapy each week. I really enjoy working with them. Adolescence is an amazing time in life. Frustrated parents ask me how long adolescence lasts. I usually reply, "Adolescence starts around 11 to 13 and it lasts an awfully long time."

When 13-year-olds tell about their new boyfriends or girlfriends, they may say, "Oh, we have so much in common. We're just alike. You know, we like the same music groups." By the next week, that relationship may have ended and they may like a different music group. No matter how major or minor musical tastes may be, at least these couples were finding out about each other's interests.

When I met Kathleen, she was a music student at SMU. She was already an accomplished pianist and violinist and played violin in the Fort Worth Symphony. I, on the other hand, took piano lessons for only one year when I was in the fifth grade.

Oh! I'll never forget my first recital. Ugh!

I was the only boy on the program with about 20 girls. Of course, being one of the "beginners," I was one of the first to play. I had practiced that sonatina what seemed like 5,000 times.

About halfway through my performance, everything in my head came to a sudden stop. My mind went blank. There was not one note in my brain. The audience was deathly silent. I placed my forehead on the keyboard in helpless defeat. After what seemed an eternity, I picked my head up and started playing the piece from its beginning—without a mistake. But the damage had already been done.

As I walked back to my seat, looking at the floor, I just wanted to run home. The rest of the recital seemed endless as all of the girls played flawlessly—at least it seemed that way to me. After the recital, the most common "compliment" I heard was, "Well, you were the best boy in the recital—ha, ha."

I struggled through one more recital and gracefully retired from the music business.

And my singing voice? It just doesn't work right. One of my Jewish friends who is a rabbi said that when you go to rabbinical school, a professor auditions new students for their singing ability. If they can sing, they become cantors. If they cannot sing, they become rabbis. Believe me, if I were Jewish, I'd be a rabbi today.

The Sunday morning after our first date, Kathleen and I attended worship on campus at Perkins Chapel. In spite of hearing me sing, Kathleen went out with me again. She has a lot of *chutzpah*.

Our musical talents and expertise were about as opposite as you can get. However, we overcame that difference. I listen to her play and sing. If I sing, I do it very softly or in the shower.

Like many couples, we also explored our other interests. Some couples are brought together because of their interests in a particular type of music, dance, sport, or hobby. One couple I know loves to race bicycles, but that is about the only interest they share. Some people enjoy mountains, while others are drawn to beaches. Some people love to shop, while others hate it. Some relish going to parties, while others prefer a quiet evening at home. Some like to skydive, while others want to keep both feet on the ground and work in the garden. Some like a lot of pets, others enjoy the freedom of no pets. Some like golf, others prefer tennis. Some like hunting and fishing, others really get into reading and photography. Some adore the opera, others like the twang of country music. Some collect modern art, others collect old baseball cards.

Participants in my study indicated interests and hobbies were more important in the earlier phases of their relationship than in the early years of their marriage. Interests and hobbies became less important the longer couples were married. Couples who had been married from two to 30 years indicated hobbies and interests were not as important in ranking as were items associated with work and career, child rearing, finances, and relationship issues. While interests and hobbies may have remained important to these couples, resources of time and money seem to have been invested elsewhere.

Combining Interests

Barry is a Civil War buff. He reads everything he can get his hands on about the War Between the States and has an extensive collection of books about the conflict. Elaine writes for a sewing publication and is an excellent seamstress herself. After attending a re-enactment of a Civil War battle, Barry discussed with Elaine his interest in participating in future re-enactments. Being the jewel she is, Elaine offered to make a Civil War uniform for her husband. Her interest in Barry's developing hobby thrilled him.

Elaine also began to attend the events with Barry. Some participants in the re-enactments contracted with Elaine to make uniforms and period pieces for them.

Same Difference

Some couples are frustrated with each other because of different levels of expertise in a hobby. A classic example is the man who wants his wife to jog or long-distance run with him, but she does not have the same interest or level of competitiveness he does.

Hank is a competitive bike rider and derives an emotional high from the sport. Because bike riding is such a thrill for him, he wanted his wife to share the same enjoyment. Penny made a few rides with Hank, but they were no fun. She said he was constantly telling her to keep pedaling *long* after she was exhausted. Penny confessed she really began to resent Hank's pushing her as though he were an Olympic coach.

After discussing the matter in our sessions, they decided Hank would continue to ride competitively with his biking friends. And they bought a tandem bike for leisurely, enjoyable rides in the neighborhood and around a nearby lake. How we deal with our similar and different interests can be critical to our relationships.

Whatever your stage in a relationship, you may benefit from identifying interests and hobbies and discussing them with your mate. How important are they to you? How can they enhance your well-being and the well-being of your relationship?

An early mentor of mine was Chaplain Dave Erb at Presbyterian Hospital in Dallas. He truly believed one of the most important questions someone could ask a potential partner was "What are your hobbies?" At that time he was a ham radio operator and had racing pigeons.

Most of us really benefit from having hobbies and interests which can stimulate our lives and relationships. It is extremely important for us to discuss each others' hobbies and interests or develop some new ones. Hobbies and interests can add spice to our lives.

Values and Beliefs

In a recent telephone conversation with our graduate student daughter, Laura, she mentioned that most of the guys she had gone out with did not have the same values she has. She is convinced that unless a guy has values and beliefs similar to hers, there is no point in pursuing a relationship with him. A person may be very attractive, have a great personality, and be a lot of fun, but the rubber begins to meet the relationship road when a couple examines and compares their values and beliefs.

Ugh and Umm believed in physical survival. Nadab and Rivka's fathers believed in social-financial unions. Julia believed in romance. Ed believed in pragmatism. What do you believe in? What is really important to you? What are your values? What are your goals? Those beliefs and values we hold sacred are important for us to discuss, understand, agree upon, or accept. In this section, we'll examine these items as they relate to you and your relationship.

Comparing and Discussing Values and Beliefs

Participants in my study indicated comparing and discussing their values and beliefs were increasingly important throughout the course of their relationships. Comparing values regarding commitment and fidelity in a relationship was rated highest; comparing their social and political values was rated lowest. Agreement was most important regarding commitment and fidelity while acceptance of social and political values was workable for most couples. For those values and beliefs you hold most dear, *agreement* between you and your mate may be most helpful to your relationship. On the other hand, those values which are of less importance may benefit simply from *acceptance* by your mate. Let's look at these issues more closely.

Acceptance

Joan is working on her master's degree in social work and has very strong feelings about most subjects: poverty, racism, sexism, homosexuality, health care, and the economy. James, her boyfriend, always looks at these subjects from what he calls a logical and practical perspective. Wow, can they have strong disagreements! She wanted him to feel the way she felt about each of these subjects—to approach them actively and with great passion. James often dismissed her "bleeding heart emotionalism" because he did not think she was being logical enough, and he always pointed out the non-passionate side of the issue. Both strongly believed they were right.

A crucial factor in dealing with value differences is *acceptance*. Acceptance does not necessarily mean that we like something—it really indicates that we acknowledge the inevitable. Disagreement was only a part of Joan and James' value difference. When each concluded they were only deepening the wedge in their relationship by trying to convince the other of their views, they began to make some progress in their relationship. Joan *accepted* that James might never have the same strong, passionate activism she has regarding various social issues. Likewise, James *accepted* that his devil's advocate logic only added fuel to their roaring disagreements.

R-E-S-P-E-C-T

When Joan and James accepted the fact that they could not change each other's minds, they called a truce. The peace was only temporary. Suddenly, another problem loomed. Each still thought the other was wrong. James admitted that although he respected Joan as a person, he did not respect her opinion. Joan grimaced, asking, "How can you say you respect me, but you don't respect my deep belief about an issue?"

Agreement and respect can be very different animals in the relationship jungle. One way to think of agreement is concurrence or being of like mind. This couple gave no indication they were willing to be animals wearing the same stripes. On the other hand, respect implies consideration or regard. If one or both people believe so strongly that agreement about particular values is crucial to their respect for the other, this is a major concern for the viability of the relationship.

In our sessions, Joan and James diligently worked on this issue because they were so committed to their relationship. After much struggle, they gained a healthy respect for each other's positions on particular issues. *This process involved their listening to each other with respectful ears rather than critical ears. They asked each other questions to gain more information and responded with thoughtful answers. In essence, they listened and shared respectfully rather than with the ears and voices of entrenched debaters.* Also, they focused on the values they agreed upon such as their basic religious beliefs, high ethical standards, honesty, and a growing respect for each other's positions on particular issues.

Politics and religion may be subjects to avoid in some situations. In intimate relationships, however, it is important to compare and discuss these and other issues respectfully. *Some of your values and beliefs may require agreement while others may need acceptance.*

If you and your mate have such strongly opposing value systems, I encourage you go through a process similar to the one that Joan and James engaged in, or seek help from a professional who can help you communicate about your differences constructively. A more thorough explanation of dealing with conflicts will be discussed in the next chapter.

The following exercise is designed to help you constructively and respectfully compare and discuss your interests, values and beliefs.

Exercise for Interests and Hobbies

(Answer these questions individually and discuss with your mate.)

1. What are your interests and hobbies?
2. How do your interests and hobbies enhance your life?
3. How do your interests and hobbies affect your relationship with your mate?
4. How can you considerately handle your different interests and hobbies?
5. What common interests do you and your mate share?
6. What other interests and hobbies might you explore or share?

Exercise for Values and Beliefs

(Be sure you are in a mood and place where you will listen and share respectfully.)

1. What are some of important values and beliefs each of you holds?
2. How well do you as a couple agree regarding your values and beliefs?
3. If there are areas of disagreement, calmly and respectfully listen to and share with each other why these values and beliefs are important to you.
4. Communicate your willingness to accept (not necessarily agree with) the other person's values and beliefs.

5. Express your appreciation to each other for calmly and respectfully sharing and listening.
6. Share with each other your values and beliefs which you hold in common.
7. What other values and beliefs will be important for you to develop or share which may enhance your lives?

Chapter 8
Are We Compatible?
Roles, Responsibilities, and Resolving Conflicts

In premarital counseling sessions, I ask couples the following question: "Of all the people you have known or dated, why do you think you can live with and why do you want to live with this person the rest of your life?" Similarly, in marital therapy, I ask couples, "Of all the people you knew or dated, why did you think you could live with and why did you want to live with this person the rest of your life?"

Compatibility is more than sociocultural factors, attraction, romance, commitment, support, and values. As important as each of these items is, being able to and wanting to live day in and day out with another person for a lifetime requires a lot of the couple. It involves the combination of the above-mentioned factors and a willingness to balance roles and responsibilities and successfully resolve issues and conflicts. In this chapter, we will explore compatibility at different stages of the relationship.

Are We Compatible Enough to Get Married?

When a couple comes to a professional with this question, there is a good likelihood that they have some questions or concerns to explore regarding their compatibility. Although compatibility may simply imply being capable of existing together, it means *much* more to have a thriving marriage.

So, what does compatibility mean to you? To explore compatibility, examine your expectations in light of these four primary questions associated with husband/wife roles.

1) *What do you expect from a mate?*

2) *What does your mate expect of you?*

3) *What do you expect of yourself as a mate?*

4) *What does your mate expect of him/herself as a mate?*

Role expectations are a complex combination of individual and interpersonal factors necessary for compatibility. Let's address role compatibility in a clear and practical manner.

Well, In My Family…

Although cultural and societal norms contribute to our role expectations in marriage, most couples report that their specific role expectations were derived from the way their own families lived their roles. Many times I've heard this righteous preface to a role expectation of a mate: "Well, in my family the man always did this and the woman always did that." Implying, "And that is the way it should be for us."

When two people from different jungles commingle, establishing role compatibility requires considerable openness, understanding, and effort. It is important for each person to share with the other how roles were lived out in their childhood households. This is not to be a presentation of how all jungles should operate, but a sharing, listening, and learning time for the couple. This awareness may be enhanced by in-house experiences with each other's families. We can draw from the experiences each of us had in our families to develop our own unique roles for compatibility.

Well, I Always Thought…

When a person seeking help regarding compatibility begins

a statement with these words, there is a strong probability that the other person is not doing what he or she wants. In addition to bringing role expectations from our families' jungles, we often bring expectations we have developed as individuals. "Well, I always thought you would...give me roses on Valentine's Day rather than candy...want to vacation with my family...want to attend my church...not mind my travel schedule...be happy for me to go to graduate school...like it if I grew a beard...want me to keep the checkbook...want to be my nephew's surrogate father."

Compatibility in Marriage

Early in a relationship, roles and responsibilities may be of little importance. But by the time a couple marries this item is becoming important. *According to my study, balancing roles and responsibilities in a marriage became the most important quality associated with compatibility*. For *some* couples, sharing fairly and balancing their roles and responsibilities is very simple and easy. For *most* couples, this is an issue requiring clear understanding and flexibility. Couples need to evaluate and discuss their views of cooperation, teamwork, and division of labor. When couples view themselves as a team rather than as entitled individuals, this spirit of cooperation will greatly enhance their compatibility. Otherwise, each person seems to feel he or she has to do everything.

Teamwork and Division of Labor

Denise is the mother of four young children. She was so frustrated because her husband, Russ, would come home to a less than perfect household and ridicule her for being lazy. She was steamed.

One day Denise wrote a list of her many chores and responsibilities. The list included such things as cook, chauffeur, maid, child care provider, gardener, accountant, tutor, lover, CEO, CFO, and COO. To each item she assigned a dollar value. Then she presented the itemized list with a concluding comment: "Pay me what I'm worth or quit complaining—or do it yourself." She got his attention.

Another stay-at-home mom, Rita, said her husband, Cody, did not understand why she was so tired when he came home from slaying dragons all day at the office. He re-emphasized the point by saying that when he kept the children for a few hours he didn't have any problems with them and they were not *that* hard to take care of.

When Rita spent ten days caring for her sister in a hospital following a serious auto accident, Cody was left to take care of everything. Rita later reported that because he was responsible for everything for more than a few hours at a time, Cody suddenly had new respect for what she did. She was sorry, of course, about her sister's accident and injuries, but she was happy that her husband had a clearer understanding about the day in, day out responsibilities she shouldered.

In some rare households, the man or woman may work all day and still do all of the cooking, cleaning and yard work, while the other is totally satisfied with the arrangement. And for many couples, the division of labor or cooperation and teamwork is an ever-changing and evolving endeavor because of work schedules, the ages and care required of children, and illness or travel.

Here are some suggestions regarding successful cooperation, teamwork and division of labor:

**Be clear about what the various responsibilities are*

**Volunteer to do your fair share*

**Check with each other to see if you have a fair division of labor*

**Be responsible and follow through with your responsibilities*
**Do some of the chores together and enjoy the camaraderie*
**Have a sense of teamwork and accomplishment*
**Express appreciation to each other for the work done*
**Relax and hug*

When couples implement their own unique workable means of handling the various responsibilities involved in carrying on a household, resentments are less likely to develop and life is just better. Discuss the responsibility equity with each other on a regular basis to see if the current system is working well or needs some refinement or change. These may seem to be such trivial matters to some of you and gravely important matters to others. Whatever your situation, just know these matters are or will become important to thriving in the household jungle.

Realistic Role Expectation

The wife of a minister expressed her frustration that her husband was pressuring her to be more active in their church. She shared in their initial counseling session that when they married her husband was in management training with an energy company. During their first four years of marriage, her husband lived the corporate life while she taught school. They lived in an upscale neighborhood where she had several close friends. She said her involvement with his job only included attending about three company events each year.

Upon responding to his call to ministry, they moved to a small town where he served a local Protestant church. While he attended classes three days a week at a seminary 50 miles away, she lived in the church's small parsonage, took care of their young child and taught English at the local high school.

Their lives had changed dramatically. They had made a

major move. They saw each other much less. Her husband had four years of seminary education ahead of him. Their income was a fraction of what it used to be. Her next-door neighbors were a herd of dairy cattle. Literally. And now her husband was expecting her to work with the youth group, be a leader in the women's organization, and be at every church function. Although she was supportive of her husband's ministry and the associated educational requirements, she was not willing to fulfill all the roles her husband was wanting her to assume.

During that first counseling session, the young minister became aware he was expecting far too much of his wife. Both had their hands full with the roles they were filling. She was their child's primary parent. As a teacher, she had many papers to read and grade, lesson plans to prepare, and school meetings and activities to attend. And she "held down the fort" seven days a week. Likewise, he felt overwhelmed by the many church responsibilities of preparing sermons, caring for parishioners, administrative duties, and adjusting to being a minister. Plus, he felt swamped by the demanding academic rigors of graduate school.

The young minister apologized to his wife for expecting so much of her. She said, "I'll pray for you, love you, support you, and attend church, but I'm not going to take on any more church responsibilities."

How realistic are your expectations of your mate? Knowing your mate the way you do, what can you honestly expect of him or her? Expecting your mate to fulfill roles he or she is unable or unwilling to perform can create frustrated feelings and undermine role compatibility. On the other hand, being considerate, clear, and realistic regarding each other's roles can contribute significantly to a couple's compatibility and help to create a much more pleasant jungle in which to coexist.

Flexibility

Although having clearly defined and agreed-upon roles is important for compatibility, flexibility is another important ingredient for continuing compatibility. As life circumstances change, it is important for couples to keep current and adjust their roles accordingly.

I grew up in a rural farming and ranching community where, for the most part, men and women's roles were stereotypically established. Even so, some of the men were quite flexible.

My mother was a public school teacher. For nine months of the year my dad cooked breakfast every morning and assumed some other roles which were traditionally female in their orientation. My mother returned to teaching a year before I started school, so my father took care of me for that year. He took me to the field each day while he plowed or planted or to the pastures while he fed the cattle. In reflection, I appreciate my parents' willingness to be flexible in the roles which facilitated more income for our family and a cooperative approach to child rearing and role compatibility.

When couples openly and lovingly *share* their expectations rather than demandingly and rigidly *present* their expectations, a major step toward compatibility is accomplished. If, however, those expectations are so important that they are unwavering and the mate is unwilling to comply, this poses a serious problem toward achieving compatibility. Whether you are early in your relationship or have been married for a long time, address these issues immediately.

Are We Still Compatible?

Many couples who have been married for some time look at each other with an uncertain expression and wonder silently—

or sometimes aloud— "Are we still compatible?" After a myriad of shared experiences, they painfully ask, "What has happened to us?"

Phillip and Mona are examples of the sad yet stereotypical couple who, after a romantic early marriage, settled into a routine of focusing on work, child rearing and individual interests. After 22 years of marriage, they had responsibly carried out their roles for their employers, children and community. But they had done a poor job of maintaining compatibility in their marital relationship.

Couples must keep current! Life's responsibilities require an amazing amount of time and energy. So, if you have been married for some time, check with each other about your current compatibility. You may need to intentionally return to some relationship roles and responsibilities which helped to create your original compatibility. Or you may discuss some updated balancing of cooperation and teamwork which would improve your compatibility. Compatibility is an ongoing and sometimes changing factor which is vital for a thriving marriage.

Exercise Regarding Roles and Responsibilities

1. How did your parents deal with roles and responsibilities when you were growing up?
2. What do you want from your mate regarding roles and responsibilities?
3. What roles and responsibilities does your mate expect of you?
4. What roles and responsibilities do you expect of yourself?
5. What roles and responsibilities does your mate expect of him/herself?
6. List the various responsibilities necessary to carry on life in your household.

(Cooking, housecleaning, grocery shopping, taking the trash out...)
7. List responsibilities each of you is willing to take. (You may want to share some of these responsibilities.)
8. Follow through with your responsibilities and feel the good feeling of accomplishment.

Dealing With Differences

Compatibility implies doing things consistently to keep the relationship running well. There are, however, those times when we need to *deal with our differences*. The following section will give practical ways to address those inevitable differences of opinion. Learning to resolve conflicts becomes crucial for couples who remain together.

Positively Resolving Conflicts

Whenever there is a difference or a conflict, we tend to get primitive. We often resort to the jungle behaviors of "fight or flight." This is survival behavior—and in such a state we are only interested in protecting ourselves. We usually develop this behavior early in our lives to survive in the jungles in which we grew up. We decided that the best way to survive was to be aggressive or to withdraw. Neither is conducive to successfully resolving conflict in a relationship. In this section we will address this crucial issue which couples rate as increasingly important for a good marriage.

WARNING! WARNING! WARNING!

Learning to positively resolve conflicts may be the single most important skill for you to possess in order to have a thriving marriage. Most of you can get along well when the road is smooth. But when the road in the jungle forks and you have different opinions about which is the right route, how do you deal with it? Here are some important truths to keep in mind regarding differences and conflict:

**Wherever two or three people are gathered together there will be conflict.* (Couples may be open about their conflict or develop ulcers instead.)

**Some people focus on being RIGHT rather than being respectful or relational.* (Is your right opinion spelled with a capital "R"?—"I'm RIGHT and you are WRONG!" Or with a lower case "r"?—"I believe I'm right, but I'm open to your opinion.")

**It is helpful to approach differences as a team focused on successfully resolving an issue.* (Rather than being adversaries entrenched in a debate.)

**There is a difference between being openly honest and brutally honest.* (Most people who are being brutally honest are often focusing more on being brutal than simply being honest.)

Here are some suggestions for successfully resolving differences:

**Ask yourself why this is a problem.*

**Be clear about the concern you have.*

**Calm yourself by taking a walk, doing something physical or meditating, and pray for yourself and your mate—and for help in resolving the issue.*

**Look into each other's eyes and hold hands as you share. Eyes and touch communicate so much.* Most couples feel less anxious and defensive when they are emotionally and physically connected.

**Or sit side by side and focus on writing the process on a sheet of paper.* This method helps couples be more objective, focus on and be clear about the issue, write brainstorming ideas, evaluate them, and select a good solution. Some couples keep a "Problem Solving Pad" on their refrigerator or desk for quick access.

I cannot emphasize too much the importance of sitting close to each other for resolving conflicts. These physical positions and points of focus will help you work together as a caring couple and a problem-solving team.

The 5 Rs to Resolving Differences in a Relationship

1) RESPECT each other.

Respect may be considered to be an attitude we have toward another or a decision we have made regarding another. Certainly implied is the fact that we also communicate respect to the other person through means of expression, words, and behaviors. That means we treat the person with high regard, honor, and consideration. When we have a difference of opinion with our mate, these attitudes, expressions, and behaviors are not always our first nature. You need to take a moment, a few minutes, or a few hours, if necessary, to remember that this is the person you chose to marry of your own free will. You may want to draw from the above list and take some deep breaths, meditate, or pray so that you will have a more respectful mindset.

You are different from your mate and it's guaranteed that you'll have some differing opinions. If you want to have a good relationship rather than engage in jungle warfare, be respectful of yourself, your mate, and your marriage. Those of us who remember Viet Nam know how long, bloody, and destructive jungle warfare can be. Instead, approach the issue with your mate with a respectful attitude so that you will greatly increase the probability of a peaceful resolution and achieve another experience in building a thriving relationship.

2) RAISE the issue in a respectful manner.

When we raise an issue by saying something like "You make me so mad..." or "You never care about me...," we are usually raising more than issues. We are also raising blood pressures, defenses, and a whole trainload of emotional freight. *Raising an issue without literally or figuratively pointing an accusing finger at our mate is vital.*

Talking in a clear and calm manner is helpful. Here are a couple of ways to raise an issue in a respectful manner. "There is something I want to talk with you about. I want to discuss it with you in a way that will be helpful to us and our relationship. Is this a good time, or would some time later be better?" Or, "I have a difference of opinion with you about something and I want to talk with you about it so that we can come to a good or workable solution for both of us."

When we have strong emotions about an issue, some of us want to resolve the problem immediately—"We've got to deal with this *right now*." Others need to take some time to sort it out in their heads—"I've got to get out of here. I'll be back *later*." Each person is feeling extremely uptight and anxious. We tend to become "primitive" in times of stress, feeling emotions which propel us to fight or flee. How can couples with these primitive instincts surging deal with issues effectively?

Keep in mind you are a team who can calm each other's anxieties. If you need some time to think through the issue, tell your more impatient mate, "I know you want to address this issue as quickly as possible—I do too. But you know me, I need some time to sort this out in my mind. Give me 15 minutes to clear my head and I'll meet you back here at 4:15 so we can deal with this issue in a way that will be good for us."

The key is giving a *specific* time which *reassures* the more impatient person that the two of you will be able to deal with the issue quickly.

If you are the more impatient party, you can thoughtfully say to your mate, "Would it help if you had a few minutes to think about this before we start to talk about the issue?" Your partner who needs some time to think will *exhale* and feel *reassured* that you are not trying to force him or her to address an issue under pressure. That's thoughtful teamwork.

These examples may seem a little unrealistic to some of you, but if you will go through the steps mentioned above, you can do it. Raise the issue keeping your mate in mind. Raise this issue as something you want to discuss in a helpful and caring manner. Raise the issue by communicating that you want to resolve the difference in a way that will be workable for both of you. Raise the issue with positive regard for your mate and a commitment to keep your cool and a caring attitude. Moreover, remember your mate and your relationship are probably more important than being right about the issue.

3) RESPOND with respect.

If your mate raises an issue, you can respond with respect by paraphrasing the issue that your mate raises with you. Although this may seem to be a somewhat artificial response to your mate, the success of resolving an issue and ensuring a thriving relationship are worth the effort.

One conflicted couple was Bruce and Bonnie. They were planning to marry, but their win-at-all-cost fights were severely damaging their relationship.

Bruce's mode of operation was to insensitively bark his decisions about an issue without considering Bonnie's opinion.

"I'm going to have a patio added to the house we're buying," he announced on their way to a premarital counseling session with me.

Bonnie furiously reacted by lecturing him about his bullheaded, inconsiderate way of making decisions which directly affected her—especially since she earned three-fourths of their income.

By the time they arrived at my office, they were debating whether they wanted to marry each other or not. After letting each of them blow off a little steam, we began to unravel the problems they were having.

Bruce admitted he just *assumed* Bonnie would view his suggestion the way he did. After all, he thought it was just logical to have the patio built before they moved in.

I suggested to Bruce that he was not the Lone Ranger with the only voice in decision-making. I told him the importance of being *aware* of Bonnie and her ideas and feelings—"You are a 'we,' not just an "I'."

After pondering my words, he grasped the point I was making and responded. "I need to be *aware* of Bonnie and *considerate* of her feelings when we have an issue to address. We are a team of two—not just a solo act."

Upon hearing Bruce's comments, Bonnie acknowledged how she, too, was selfish far too often when they had different opinions.

Bruce apologetically looked at his fiancée and softly said, "Bonnie, I'm sorry I was so inconsiderate this evening when I *told* you about *my* patio idea."

Bonnie gently touched his hand, accepted his apology and told him she was sorry for *reacting* to his idea with such hurtful comments.

Bruce smilingly said, "Bonnie, I'd like to take another stab at this issue. I would like to talk with you about the possibility of adding a patio to the home we plan to buy. I'd like to discuss this with you right now, if that would be all right with you."

Bonnie, grinning and knodding her head affirmatively,

said, "Let's talk about it."

When couples raise an issue and respond respectfully, they have made the biggest step toward resolving an issue peacefully. And when a person raises an issue in the manner described above, the respondent will usually reply in a caring, respectful manner. Sometimes people may be so pleasantly surprised at the thoughtful manner in which their mates raise the issue that they will say, "Wow! I liked that! Now what is it you would like to talk about?" Or, "Tell me about it and I'll bet we can work this out."

4) RESOLVE the issue.

So many unresolved issues can create deeply hurt feelings, brick walls of defenses, or dams of resentment. Without resolution, issues are like wounds or sores which may or may not remain open, but can become infected and pose greater danger to the health of the person. If, however, couples raise issues and respond respectfully, then focus on a mutually agreeable understanding or solution, this helps to build trust in each other and confidence in resolving differences. Resolving an issue brings about healing within each person in the relationship.

5) REJOICE!

When a couple resolves an issue, it is cause for celebration. It is a major accomplishment for a great cause—the cause of two special people in a unique relationship who want a fulfilling, loving, intimate, lifetime, thriving marriage. So, shake hands, hug, or kiss, but certainly congratulate each other. Be joyful.

A Process for Resolving Issues

With the 5 Rs as a foundation, here's a simple step-by-step way to tackle your issues.

**Identify the issue.* Be clear within yourself what the issue is and communicate it clearly and respectfully to your mate.

**Agree on the issue.* By paraphrasing and clarifying, agree what the issue is.
**Propose possible solutions either together or separately.* Some couples enjoy brainstorming ideas together. This synergistic experience can be creative, productive, and sometimes humorous. Other couples find they are more productive when they separately compile a list of possible solutions.
**Select a solution that will be good for the relationship.* The focus must not be on "my way or no way," "my solution is better than yours," "I'm right and you're wrong," or "the solution must be perfect." Approach the solution as a team selecting a good, considerate, workable solution.
**Follow through or implement the solution.* Simply said: Do what you agree to do.
**Re-evaluate the solution.* Respectfully and considerately check with each other to determine whether the solution is working or not. If not, begin with step one.
**Congratulate each other.*

Exercise for Positively Resolving Conflicts

1. How did your parents deal with and resolve differences and conflicts?
2. Share with each other areas in which you want to improve so that you will be able to more successfully resolve conflicts. (Not yell, not withdraw, etc.)
3. Review and discuss the 1) thoughts about conflict, 2) suggestions for resolving conflicts, 3) the 5 Rs, and 4) the process of resolving conflicts.
4. Commit to raise, respond to and resolve issues respectfully.
5. Rejoice!

Chapter 9
Thriving in the Garden of Marriage: Together, Intimately, and With Great Sex

Companionship

One of the thoughts frequently expressed by couples in a thriving relationship is that they really enjoy being together. These couples are not dependent upon activities or events for good times. Rather, they are more relationship-oriented. They really, truly enjoy each other's company without having to *do* something.

In fact, married couples ranked companionship in third place overall behind emotional support and commitment and fidelity as the most important factor in their relationships. Women ranked it as very important from their first meeting; men said it was somewhat. Frequent descriptions by women included: "I really enjoyed his company"..."I felt very comfortable with him"..."We just talked and talked—and it seemed we could talk forever" and "I felt close to him." Men's comments included: "I felt very comfortable with her"... "It was easy to talk with her"... "I felt like I could tell her anything and everything" and "I enjoyed just being with her."

During their courtship, women ranked companionship as the second most important quality in their relationship. And by the time the coupled married, both men and women ranked companionship only behind commitment and fidelity in importance. Companionship continued to be one of the most important qualities for a thriving relationship throughout the course of the marriage.

The evidence from couples in my study indicates that being comfortable with and enjoying spending time with a mate are vital for a thriving marriage. Other statements from couples which described their sense of companionship included: "We are very close to each other"... "He's so easy to talk with"... "I just love her more and more as the years go by"... "We are best friends"... "We can spend times without saying a word to each other and just smile when we look at each other"... "We'd rather be with each other than with anyone else"... "We enjoy the good times with each other and we are there for each other in the hard times"... "We are soul mates" and "We laugh a lot."

Whether you're dating, engaged, newly married, or married for a long time, being in a relationship which mirrors the above descriptions will help you feel that you are living in a serene and beautiful garden, rather than in an uncomfortable or even hostile jungle. I remember an older couple who held hands as they described what companionship was for them. Theirs was a relationship which included mutual acceptance, a graceful flow to their conversation, a grounded sense of security, and a peaceful knowing that had helped and would continue to help them to walk confidently as best friends through challenging jungles or blissful gardens.

Alone, Together, Intimate

One of the ways to help facilitate companionship if you are not in perfect sync with each other is to develop a clear and workable understanding of each other's desires to be alone, together, and intimate. The following is an example of a couple who came to me with quite different needs in these areas. But they were able to address them in ways which helped to create a greater degree of companionship.

Greg grew up on a ranch in Montana and needed a lot of alone time. His image of alone was that he would be in the wide open spaces of Montana or Wyoming while his wife was back home in Texas or with her family in Boston. Conversely, Carla's image of alone was quite different. For her, alone meant that after working all day at an accounting firm, she would "play" in the kitchen while Greg would "play" in the garage working on a project.

Their true story becomes even more interesting.

For Greg, together meant spending time together at home. He would be in the garage woodworking while Carla did her thing in the kitchen. On the other hand, Carla's idea of being together was sitting on the sofa together, snuggling while they watched a movie.

You knew it.

For Greg, intimate meant sitting on the sofa snuggling and watching a movie while for Carla, intimate meant making love.

Greg needed a lot of alone time and Carla wanted a lot of together and intimate time.

After some serious and sometimes humorous negotiations, Greg and Carla agreed on a model that would work for them. One week of their two weeks' vacation would be spent with Greg alone in Montana while Carla would spend that time with her family and friends in Boston. Both agreed to a combination of together time in the garage and kitchen or on the sofa. Furthermore, both agreed to intimacy which included both snuggling and lovemaking times.

A key to the success of these agreements was that both Greg and Carla used the 5 Rs method described in the previous chapter to resolve their differences. That helped them develop a workable and fulfilling sense of compatibility.

Sex in the Garden

Some of you may have been wondering when we were going to get to sex. Well, here it is. Of course volumes have been and can be written on the subject. However, this section will simply address sex based on the findings from my study and some helpful suggestions for its contribution to a thriving marriage.

Not surprisingly, having a satisfying and fulfilling sex life was very important for men from their first meeting with the women who became their spouses. This item was ranked considerably lower by men than physical attractiveness and sexual attraction at their initial meeting. By the time couples married, having a satisfying and fulfilling sex life was *extremely* important for men and *very* important for women. During the course of marriage, the importance of sex dropped somewhat. Its importance, however, was still rated very highly by both men and women, with men rating it somewhat higher than women. It is important to note that *satisfying* and *fulfilling* were key descriptors of the sexual relationship.

Fore-Foreplay

In most couples one partner wants sex more often than the other. That's a fact of life. When it's a man who wants sex more often, a common complaint of the female partner or spouse is that her partner or husband starts foreplay by grabbing and squeezing, which is often unappreciated and insensitive. When it's a woman who wants sex more often, a common complaint of the male partner or spouse is that his partner or wife doesn't understand that when he grabs and squeezes her he's just trying to let her know he finds her sexy.

To set up terrific sex, one term I introduce to couples is "fore-foreplay." In essence, fore-foreplay is how you treat your mate the minute, hour, day, week, or month before you start actual foreplay. Here are some fore-foreplay suggestions:

Non-sexual hugging

Soft kisses

Tender conversation

Gentle touch (non-sexual)

Giving cards, letters or flowers

Writing a poem for your mate (This does not have to be Shakespeare!)

Having a romantic date

Considerate actions, such as cleaning the kitchen, washing your mate's car, or cooking dinner

Listening attentively

Expressing appreciation and affection

Just being nice to your mate and sensitive to her or his feelings, rather than leading with sex

Good Sex is Good Communication

Whether the communication is verbal ("not now," "yes," "more gentle," or "let's go to the bedroom") or non-verbal (smile, frown, pat on the shoulder, or embrace), it can contribute greatly to thriving or simply surviving sexually. At non-sex times, openly and lovingly share with each other what you would like and not like sexually. Even if you have had a sexual relationship for a long time, it is a good idea to discuss each other's sexual likes and dislikes.

Because many people feel very vulnerable when talking about sex, being very considerate of each other's feelings is crucial. Raise these concerns gently and lovingly. When a person says "You never (or always) want to have sex," you can bet the couple's sex life is not going to improve quickly. Such comments are guaranteed to shut down intimacy and build up walls.

Both men and women indicate that having a satisfying and fulfilling sex life is very important to a thriving marriage. Here are some suggestions couples in my study offered to enhance sexual fulfillment:

**Be considerate enough to ask what I would like*
**Listen carefully to my intimate suggestions; share with me what you would like*
**Let's experiment*
**A weekend getaway*
**Safety and security with excitement*
**Be romantic*
**Be playful and uninhibited*
**Be sensitive and considerate*
**Enjoy*
**Have fun*
**Be gentle*
**Be patient and don't rush*
**Be sensual*
**Be sexual*
**Be intimate*

If you need help in your sex life, be resourceful by reading books, talking with a trusted person, or going to a therapist or physician who has expertise in dealing with sexual issues. Unfortunately, many people have had painful sexual experiences as children, adolescents, or adults. Others have had unhealthy or cruel emotional messages about sex given to them from the jungles of misguided parents, pornography, perverted people, or warped religion.

"My Sunday School Teacher Said It Was a Sin, Then Mom Said It Was a Duty"

Sad but true, some people are given horrible messages about sex. Throughout her growing up years, Marilyn attended, as she described, a "rigid and severe" church with her family. She also described her Sunday School teacher during most of those years as a "rigid and severe" woman who warned them about the evils of sex. She vividly remembered this woman telling the girls' class: "Sex is a sin and you know what happens to people who sin!" Marilyn knew clearly what the teacher was saying: "If I have any type of sexual experience, it is a sin. And I will go straight to hell."

Then, before Marilyn and Bart got married, her mother gave her more disturbing information about sex. While buttoning her wedding dress, Marilyn's mom told her that women have to *endure* sex, that she would not get any pleasure from it, only men enjoy it, but it was her *duty* to have sex with her husband.

No wonder Marilyn and Bart had problems with their sex life.

Every time Marilyn had sex, she felt guilty and had never had a pleasurable sexual experience. This frightened, yet courageous and bright young woman made a strong commitment to overcome her "sexual hang-ups."

I'm the Boss of My Body

Marilyn chose as her first therapy goal to develop a more positive and healthy attitude about her body image. Although she reported being 20 pounds overweight, Bart said he found his wife to be very sexy and attractive. Still, Marilyn felt ashamed of her body and would not undress in her husband's presence unless the room was dark. Her thoughts were, "I don't like my body...I cannot love my body."

To change this negative image, Marilyn was open to becoming "thankful" for her body. "At least I'm healthy...and it functions well," she timidly admitted.

Marilyn went home that night and began her prayerful "I'm thankful" ritual. She felt comfortable looking at her hands and fingers and being thankful for them. Over the next days, Marilyn addressed each body part with awareness and thanksgiving. She even wrote about these experiences in a journal. Once she humorously confessed, "I'm even thankful for my elbows. Aren't they truly incredible hinges!"

At the next session, Marilyn said, "Well, I'm doing much better about my body image. But now I'm down to my private parts—and that seems to be the hardest."

She painfully recalled her first bra-buying conversation with her mom. "My mom told me in a disgusted tone that I needed to get a bra to cover up those 'things.' And we never had a talk about my having a period or about my menstrual cycle. Never!" Tears poured from Marilyn's eyes. "I don't want these experiences to control how I feel about my body," she cried.

I invited Marilyn to picture her mother sitting in a chair in my office and to tell her how she really felt. Marilyn emotionally expressed her feelings of shame, hurt, and anger. Finally she concluded that this was *her* body to be thankful for and to celebrate—not her mother's property to condemn. What a marvelous and accurate revelation.

Marilyn and Bart have a four-year-old daughter and a six-year-old son. So I shared a personal story with them to anchor her decision about taking ownership of her own body. The story involved my own daughter, Laura.

When Laura was almost four, she attended our church's preschool. While driving her home from school one day, I asked that proverbial parent question: "What did you do at school today?" She said that their teacher had talked with them about not letting people touch your private parts. I was not sure what she understood that to mean, so I asked her what that meant to her.

She pondered my question for a few moments.

Then, she sat up straight in her child safety seat with her little hands forming fists and declared, "That means I'm the boss of my body!" As a parent, I thought that was great. By the way, she is now 23 years old and she's *still* the boss of her body.

This story had special meaning for Marilyn as she took ownership of her body and changed her way of thinking about her sexuality.

But What About Having Sex?

Marilyn's next issue to address was the "sin of having sex" message from her childhood Sunday School teacher and the "enduring sex" message from her mom.

In this session, Marilyn pictured both the Sunday School teacher and her mom on the sofa in my office. For the next 45 minutes, Marilyn released a lifetime of emotional pain, guilt, shame, and anger. She let go of the sex warnings from the rigid and severe Sunday School teacher and the dreadful advice from her sexually grim mother. She concluded by powerfully exclaiming: "I will not allow your emotionally, sexually, and spiritually abusive messages about having sex to control my sex life with Bart any more. I may not have all the answers yet, but with some help, Bart and I are going to do all we can to have a great sex life."

Through each of these sessions, Bart was a very supportive partner. He also worked on his own views of sex. Because of his love, sensitivity, and patience, Marilyn began to trust herself and Bart enough for them to begin developing a touching, caressing, intimate, and growing sexual relationship.

The images we have of sex as being sinful, dirty, perverted, fun, private, exploitive, sacred, pleasurable, loving, natural, unnatural, everything, or nothing contribute heavily to our expressions with our mate. Some people are scared of sex while others are very comfortable. Some people are obsessed by it while others avoid it.

What is your image of sex? How do you view it physically, mentally, emotionally, and spiritually? What is your attitude about sex?

Sex is a Gift

When sex is treated as a wonderful gift to have, to give, and to receive, it truly can be satisfying and fulfilling. There is not much room in a thriving relationship for selfish sex. Thrive in the joy of giving sexual pleasure to your mate in ways that he or she finds most fulfilling.

Sometimes sex may *only* be about having an orgasm or ejaculating. Most couples report that being able to help each other experience this physical, sexual ecstasy is one of their most enjoyable and *satisfying* gifts to each other.

"Having sex" was portrayed by persons in my research as:

*"Fast and fun."

*"High octane sensuality."

*"Playful."

*"Direct and to the point."

*"A great release."

*"Just plain sexy."

*"That great orgasmic experience."

Some couples, however, described sexual *fulfillment* as *love-making*. Words used to describe lovemaking included by people in my research are:

*"Incredible closeness."

*"I really feel loved."

*"A head-to-toe sensual experience."

*"Intimacy in the highest form."

*"When we take the time to truly make love, the intimacy is heightened to a spiritual level."

*"It takes more time, but it's worth it."

*"My wife likes it a lot more than a quickie...and so do I."

Whether you are having sex or making love, these are gifts which benefit from appropriate and considerate fore-foreplay. This remarkable ingredient of fore-foreplay helps the couple to experience satisfaction and fulfillment while engaging in sex and lovemaking. How about spending *a lot* of your time together in playful, loving fore-foreplay? When sex and lovemaking are shared as loving gifts, they are significantly more satisfying and fulfilling. And they leave a wonderful feeling which we want to experience again and again.

You might consider great sex and great lovemaking as mental, emotional, and spiritual experiences. Together, they include the thinking and emotions of the mind, the physical and sexual feelings of the body, and the intimacy and sharing of the spirit.

Wow!—an orgasm of the mind, body, and spirit!

Have great sex. Make great love. Satisfy. Fulfill. Thrive in the garden.

Dealing with Children

This is a book about mate selection and marriage rather than about child rearing. However, if you have children or plan to have children, they are or will be a significant part of your life together. Couples in the study who had children from babies to adults indicated that *how* they as a couple deal with their child or children is *very* important for their good relationship.

I could not tell you the number of parents I have heard frustratedly lament that they wished they had discussed child rearing philosophies and practices before they had married. So often the different jungles of child rearing practices husbands and wives come from powerfully affect the children, the marriage, and the family as a whole. Therefore, this section will not focus on particular child rearing practices, but specifically on how the couple deals with their child or children.

The Importance of Parents Being United

Whether you are dating, engaged, married with children, or planning to have children, by all means discuss with your mate your thoughts about child rearing as openly and respectfully as possible. Almost every week I see adolescents, couples, or families in circumstances in which the parents are in strong disagreement about how to deal with their child. Often one parent is very strict and punitive while the other parent is easygoing and lenient. This combination of approaches to parenting is almost guaranteed to produce conflict, hurt feelings, resentment, and confusion.

As a parent, I urge you to read books on parenting and discuss them. Attend parenting classes. Discuss parenting with couples whose parenting styles you admire. Share with each other how your parents dealt with you at different ages.

When you have differences about child rearing, use the 5 Rs method to respectfully raise, respond to, and resolve your differences. Then, when dealing with your children, you can be united. Not united *against* the children. But united as a couple in how you can most clearly, consistently, and considerately deal with your children and the many situations parents encounter. Your child or children and your marriage will greatly benefit.

One further suggestion which may be helpful for parents is to think developmentally. This book is a developmental model of the process of mate selection and marriage. Also, we know that children are developing human beings. It is crucial for us as parents to continue developing. This does not mean that we need to change our values and beliefs. It simply means that parenting styles must necessarily change along with the changing age of the child. And each child is uniquely different.

You must deal with each child as a unique individual so that you can facilitate the development of that person in a way that is most beneficial. We of course need to be fair and consistent, but our children are not all made from the same mold. They are always different, sometimes *very* different.

Parenting is undoubtedly one of the most amazing, frustrating, enjoyable, scary, delightful, expensive, rewarding, tiring, educational, and incredible experiences we ever have in life. I cannot encourage you enough to share these experiences with your mate in a considerate, open, loving, and united manner. Doing so will allow you to survive tough parental times and thrive in joyful parental times together as a team.

Having Fun

One of the shiny, bright facets couples often reveal in their comments about companionship is that they have a lot of fun with each other. Fun is one of those special qualities which is unique to each person or couple. It is certainly different things to different people. Couples reported fun to be: playing bridge, building a house together, going to horse shows, taking walks together, traveling, sitting on the deck, watching favorite movies, spending weekends at different bed and breakfasts, visiting their grandchildren, visiting family or friends, playing golf, telling jokes to each other, remembering past experiences, planning their future, snow skiing, water skiing, dancing, going to circuses, going to zoos, and working in the garden. Different strokes for different folks.

When Kathleen and I were dating, we were students without much money. So one of our fun times was walking to a grocery store, selecting and buying the best avocado we could find, bringing it back to the dorm or going to a park, cutting that avocado in half and eating it. It was an experience we still remember with fondness. During those inexpensive "avocado times" we laughed a lot and had a good time.

One couple in their 60s who came to me admitted they continue to have fun by jumping out of the shower naked and announcing to the other in a loud, lyrical voice "Ta Da!" Even in their self described "aging, sagging, and overweight state," they still laugh each time this occurs.

When I see couples in therapy, I often ask them to rate their fun on a 0 to 10 scale. *Fun may not be the most crucial element for remedying a relationship crisis, but it is often a good barometer of the health and happiness of the relationship*. How would you rate the fun in your relationship on such a scale?

Most couples in my study indicated that they would not have married their mates if they had not had fun with them. Furthermore, most married couples stated that having fun helped them to be good companions. One man acknowledged, "It certainly helps to have a good sense of humor, to be able to laugh at yourself, and to laugh with your mate. If you can do those things often, you can make it through most things and have a lot of fun in the process. It has certainly helped me and my wife in our 47 years together."

To have a thriving relationship—have fun!

Exercise for Companionship

1. What do you enjoy about each other's company?
2. What helps you feel compatible with your mate?
3. What helps (or would help) you to be best friends?

Exercise for Alone, Together and Intimate

1. Share with each other your description of being alone.
2. Share with each other your description of being together.
3. Share with each other your description of being intimate.
4. Discuss ways that you can considerately accommodate each other's needs to be alone, together and intimate.

Exercise for Sex and Lovemaking

1. Share with each other the messages about sex you had in your growing up years and their implications for your current views of sex.
2. What kinds of fore-foreplay does each of you like?
3. Share openly and lovingly what you would like and not like sexually.
4. Share your thoughts about the physical aspects of sex.
5. Share your thoughts about the mental aspects of sex.
6. Share your thoughts about the emotional aspects of sex.
7. Share your thoughts about the spiritual aspects of sex.
8. Discuss what helps (or would help) your sex life to be more satisfying.
9. Discuss what helps (or would help) your lovemaking to be more fulfilling.
10. Remember that sex and lovemaking are shared loving gifts.

Exercise for Dealing With Children

1. Share with each other how your parents dealt with you when you were growing up.
2. What are your views about parenting?
3. What are you views about discipline?
4. How can you and your mate be more united in how you parent?

Exercise for Fun

1. Rate how much fun you have together on a 0 to 10 scale.
2. Discuss ways you have fun together.
3. What could you do to have even MORE spice and fun in your relationship?

Chapter 10
Continuing In the Garden for a Lifetime: Money, Values, and Faith

The Same Things Are Important, Just Keep Doing Them

We are all aware of marriages that end in divorce after 20, 30, or even 40 years. What may have been a good relationship in its earlier years ends very tragically. What can we do to keep our marriages thriving in the continuing jungles we journey through? In this concluding chapter, we address this question regarding a thriving, lifetime marriage.

Among the most interesting findings from my study was that in spite of the numerous historical and societal changes which have occurred during the decades from the 40s through the 90s, *couples married during the past six decades consistently agreed about the factors most important in mate selection and marriage.* Husbands and wives who have been married from 56 years to two months are in *strong agreement* about these items for relationship development. Although continuous adjustments are necessary due to changing lifestyles in a lengthy relationship spanning several decades, the subjects discussed in this book are essential for a meaningful, solid, growing, intimate marriage.

Continuing Companionship

One of my favorite ways of thinking about life is that it is a journey. And without a doubt, our most important intimate relationship is a journey as well. From a couple's first glance or exchange, through their development and maturity, they become remarkable travelers.

When each Adam and Eve or Ugh and Umm met, they really had no idea what kinds of jungles and gardens they would journey through. That isn't the case for couples who married at the start of the World War II era right on through couples who'll marry in the 21st century. *For all the couples in those six decades, the qualities that are important in mate selection, relationship development and marriage are the same.* This revelation is both comforting and profound. Comforting in knowing that the same qualities for thriving intimate relationships endure from generation to generation. Profound in being able to pinpoint with great certainty what is really important in selecting a mate, developing an intimate relationship and having a lifetime thriving marriage.

"I Want a Marriage Like You and Grandpa Had"

Evelyn was in my office recently because she was grieving over the recent death of her husband of 56 years. She felt so lost without him. She felt so lonely and sad. Her most worrisome concerns, however, were for her 26-year-old granddaughter. The granddaughter's mom, Evelyn's daughter, had gone though a sordid divorce during the year Evelyn's husband was terminally ill. Evelyn's granddaughter had been severely affected by the mid-life crisis of her father, his affair with a woman younger than herself, his having a baby by this young woman, and his having nothing to do with his adult daughter or son.

Evelyn stated that she wished she could help her granddaughter to have a close, loving, lifetime marriage like she and her husband had. I suggested that she talk with her granddaughter about her concern.

The next week when Evelyn came in for her session, she reported she and her granddaughter did have a talk. Smiling through her tears she described the conversation in this way: "My granddaughter told me that she loved me and her grandfather so much and that we had been her role models of character and a good marriage. She said, 'I want a marriage where there is commitment, faithfulness, love, consideration, mutual support, fun, and respect for each other...like yours and Grandpa's marriage.'" Her granddaughter had touched her heart with these words.

Evelyn had married in 1942. Her granddaughter would not marry until the 21st century. Both wanted the same qualities in a marriage.

Agreeing About Money

One bit of advice that Evelyn shared with her granddaughter was "be sure that you and your future husband talk about and agree on money matters." *Sooner or later, money is an issue for almost every couple.* Although I do not claim to be a financial expert, the following addresses money issues from a relationship perspective.

I frequently ask couples to evaluate areas pertaining to financial matters on a 0 to 10 scale. Example: On a 0 to 10 scale, with 10 being best, how would you (or each of you) rate your earnings? Ten means that you earn enough money. Of course most people wish they had more. But how would you score earnings? Next, rate on a 0 to 10 scale how well you agree about spending money. Finally, rate on a 0 to 10 scale how well you agree about saving, investing and giving money. You may score each of the three items separately.

Once a couple has written their individual scores, we compare them for similarity and difference. Then I ask each person to share what their individual scores mean and their comments about each.

Not only are we talking about money, we are looking at HOW they are addressing the subject and each other. Respectfully? Openly and honestly? With much frustration? In an agreeing manner? From opposite viewpoints? Then we use the 5 Rs method to resolve issues they have.

Some vitally important money-related topics resulting from real-life discussions with clients include:

**Sharing openly and honestly with each other about income, savings and debts*
**Developing an agreeable budget*
**Deciding who will pay the bills (one or both together)*
**Deciding about expenditures over a certain amount requiring joint agreement*
**Agreeing about joint, separate or joint and separate accounts*
**Having weekly, bi-monthly or monthly financial meetings to keep current and to be clear about balances, expenditures and financial issues*
**Establishing a savings plan*
**Having a trustworthy consultant for financial advice*
**Taking classes about personal financial issues*
**Developing an investment plan*
**Deciding about life insurance*
**Having a will prepared*
**Agreeing about contribution to religious organizations, charities, etc.*
**Setting aside money for entertainment, travel, and fun*

Some couples fight about money. Others avoid dealing with financial issues. Both methods are destructive to the financial well-being of the couple as well as to their relationship. Whatever your financial or relationship status may be, HOW you discuss money will be important.

Most couples in my study indicated they did not discuss thoroughly or address financial issues until *after* they married. Money may not be the most romantic topic, but as a friend of mine from college was fond of saying, "Love may make the world go around, but money greases the wheel."

If you are in a serious dating relationship, money is a must topic to discuss. If you are engaged, discuss it NOW. If you are married, discuss it NOW. When you discuss money, keep in mind to be respectful and considerate so that money can grease the wheel of your loving relationship rather than throw a wrench into the gears causing friction and destruction.

The Jungles and Gardens of Values and Religious Beliefs

In her state of grief, Evelyn admitted her faith helped her to survive the loss of her husband. She also said that what was important to one had been important to the other. "Our faith and what we believed in helped to hold us together all those years," she declared.

While continuing to discuss and compare values and religious beliefs remains important to married couples, how they *practice* or *live* their values and beliefs becomes even more important during marriage. Discussing and comparing seem to provide a deep level of conversation for couples as well as a means of "keeping current" with each other as one's values and beliefs may change little or dramatically over the years. For example, as you age you may have become more conservative about some values or religious beliefs while you may have become more liberal about others. The key is being able to discuss openly and respectfully with your mate your values about what is right and wrong, good and bad, just and unjust, responsible and irresponsible.

The Practice of Values

As important as being able to discuss values and beliefs, it is even more important how couples practice their values and beliefs. It is, for example, very difficult to live with a person very long if they do not tell the truth and are not trustworthy. In an earlier chapter the values of commitment and fidelity were rated by married couples as most important at the present time in their marriage. These are values that must be carried out behaviorally and consistently, not just given lip service.

Although couples are bound to have some differences in their values, the more compatible or in agreement they are the better. Such couples will have fewer issues that nag, bother, or are downright unacceptable to each other. Two points are very import here: 1) In mate selection, finding a mate with similar values will greatly enhance the development of the relationship, and 2) In marriage, respectfully discussing and keeping up to date with each other's developing value systems will help the marriage to thrive rather than simply survive.

The Practice of Religious Beliefs

You have probably heard a story about a woman who is very religious and is very active in her church or synagogue. Her husband, however, never participates with her in any of the religious services. She prays and prays that one day her husband will join her for worship. Because they never share in the practice or active participation of faith, a separation exists in that marriage that ranges from being mildly frustrating to deeply painful. This story illustrates the challenges for couples who disagree about religion.

Minimal Practice in Religious Groups

Both husbands and wives in my study indicate that *how*

they practice their religious beliefs is very important. This means different things to different couples.

For some couples, how they practice their religious beliefs simply means that they agree to not participate in religious activities or to only attend religious services at Christmas and Easter or Hanukkah and Passover.

For other couples, how they practice their religious beliefs means that they have the same or similar religious affiliations—such as Protestant, Catholic, or Jewish—even though they have little or no active involvement in a religious group.

Other couples are somewhat more specific by saying that they are both Baptists, Methodists, Presbyterians, Lutherans, Episcopalians, Disciples of Christ, Church of Christ, Nazarenes, Non-denominational, Unitarians, or Reform Jews. While these couples hold particular religious beliefs, they usually participate minimally in the religious groups of which they are members.

In each of these above responses, the couples' emphasis was not about their active practice or participation in their particular religion. Rather, there were two main points of note: For some couples, their agreement was about their lack of or minimal level of participation in religious activities and other couples point to agreeing about their particular religious group's beliefs. In both cases, it is the couple's *agreement* that is key to *how* they practice their faith.

Although couples in these groups do not consider themselves to be *active* in their religious groups, they indicate that their faith is important to them and that they do identify themselves with a particular religious group's beliefs. Also, although the practice of their beliefs may not be closely associated with their active participation in religious activities, they do indicate that they practice their beliefs in the way they live their lives.

Active Participants in Religious Groups

A second group of couples concerning the practice of religious beliefs state that agreeing about being active in their religious groups is very important. These levels of agreement range from regular attendance of worship services to committed involvement in bible studies, Sunday school classes, men's and women's groups, prayer groups, service groups, or being leaders in their churches or synagogues. In these cases, *how* they practice their religious beliefs focuses on their agreement to have active involvement and their *shared* experiences in these activities.

When Religious Beliefs Are Essential

Although similar to the group just discussed, a third group is couples who indicate that the practice of their religious beliefs is important, if not crucial, for their marriage surviving and/or thriving. These people passionately relate how their deep faith, prayer life and shared religious activities and experiences help them to survive the struggles and challenges in their lives. They state their religious togetherness helps them to thrive in the joys and blessings of their lives. Many of these couples also state that their faith and marriages were significantly affected by their joint participation in couples' groups and in marriage seminars and retreats.

Continuing to Survive and Thrive

Couples who are able to survive in the jungles and thrive in the gardens of their marriages agree on many things, including values and religious beliefs. Realistically, we all know that there are numerous challenges and pains we experience in life and in all relationships, including marriage. Sometimes, simply surviving those times is a major accomplishment. But being able to *thrive* is what we want to do as much as we can.

How can we survive and thrive in this incredible journey of marriage? This book has given you ideas, information, exercises, and an army of tools you can use to help you have a good, loving, intimate, fulfilling, thriving, lifetime marriage.

Remember, couples who:

**are faithful and committed to each other*
**give emotional support and encouragement to each other*
**enjoy being with each other*
**express appreciation and affection to each other*
**agree about roles and responsibilities*
**effectively resolve their differences and conflicts*
**agree about values and religious beliefs*
**like each other's personalities*
**are physically and sexually attracted to each other*
**have a satisfying and fulfilling sex life*
**agree about how to deal with their children*
**develop an agreeable way to deal with financial issues*
**can share their thoughts and feelings and listen to each other*

have been thriving in marriages through the decades and will continue to do so.

Exercise Regarding Financial Issues

1. On a 0 to 10 scale, rate:
Your earnings (10 means you earn enough money)_____
How well you agree about spending money_____
How well you agree about savings_____, investing_____, giving_____
2. Compare your scores and discuss your similarities and differences.

3. Refer to the text for suggestions for dealing with financial issues such as:
Do you have a workable budget? If not, develop one.
Who pays the bills and how?
Do you have weekly or regular financial meetings?
Do you have a savings plan?
Do you have a trusted friend or professional to discuss financial matters?
Do you have an investment plan?
Do you have adequate life insurance?
Do you have a will?
Do you agree about contributions and giving?
Do you set aside money for entertainment, travel, and fun?

Exercise Regarding Values

1. List some of your most important values.
2. How are your values similar to and different from those of your mate?
3. How can you most effectively deal with your value differences?
4. Celebrate the values you have in common.

Exercise Regarding Religious Beliefs

1. Discuss how you agree and disagree about religious beliefs.
2. Discuss how you want to practice your religious beliefs.
3. Discuss how active you want to be in your church or synagogue.
4. Share how your faith is important in your personal life.
5. Discuss how important you want your faith to be in your marriage.
6. When have you felt closest to God?

7. Discuss some of your faith struggles.
8. Discuss how you want to grow spiritually.
9. Pray for your mate every day.
10. Pray for yourself every day so that you can be the husband or wife your mate needs you to be and God wants you to be.

The Final Exercise

Review, discuss and share your thoughts, feelings, and commitments regarding:

1. Being faithful and committed to each other.
2. Giving emotional support and encouragement to each other.
3. Enjoying being with each other.
4. Expressing appreciation and affection to each other.
5. Agreeing about roles and responsibilities.
6. Effectively resolving differences and conflicts.
7. Agreeing about how to deal with children.
8. Having an agreeable plan to deal with financial matters.
9. Sharing thoughts and feelings and listening to each other.
10. Sharing and agreeing about values and religious beliefs.
11. Liking each other's personalities.
12. Being physically and sexually attracted to each other.
13. Having satisfying sex and fulfilling lovemaking.
14. Doing these items consistently, intentionally, and lovingly.
15. Using the following list for regular check-ups to ensure a thriving marriage.

CONCLUSION

For Your Current or Future Thriving Relationship…

The following pages contain a relationship scale I developed to help couples evaluate their relationships. I strongly encourage you to use this tool now, or monthly, or every six months or certainly as an anniversary check-up. Honestly and respectfully evaluate yourself and your mate regarding how well you are doing. Then thoughtfully share, discuss, commit to improve in some areas, and celebrate those areas where you thrive or swing in the treetops.

PARSONS RELATIONSHIP SCALE FOR A THRIVING MARRIAGE

Rate each item which applies on a 0 to 10 scale* and write that number in the blank.

There is a space for your number and that of your mate.

Today's date:___________________

Initials of each person: _____ _____

1. I am faithful and committed to my mate. _____ _____
My mate is faithful and committed to me. _____ _____
2. I give emotional support and encouragement to my mate. _____ _____
My mate gives emotional support and encouragement to me. _____ _____
3. I really enjoy being with my mate. _____ _____
My mate really enjoys being with me. _____ _____
4. I lovingly express appreciation and affection to my mate. _____ _____
My mate lovingly expresses appreciation and affection to me. _____ _____
5. I am physically and sexually attracted to my mate. _____ _____
My mate is physically and sexually attracted to me. _____ _____
6. We considerately balance our roles and responsibilities. _____ _____
7. We effectively deal with and resolve our conflicts. _____ _____

8. We agree about how to deal with children. _____ _____
Or, we agree to have or not to have children. _____ _____
9. We agree about how to deal with financial matters. _____ _____
10. I openly share my thoughts and feelings with my mate. _____ _____
My mate openly shares thoughts and feelings with me. _____ _____
11. I really listen well to my mate. _____ _____
My mate really listens well to me. _____ _____
12. We share, accept and agree about values. _____ _____
13. We share, accept and agree about religious beliefs. _____ _____
14. We share in and agree about religious practices. _____ _____
15. I really like my mate's personality. _____ _____
16. We have a satisfying sex life. _____ _____
17. We have fulfilling lovemaking. _____ _____
18. We agree about how to deal with each other's families. _____ _____
19. We agree about work and career matters. _____ _____
20. I pray every day for my mate, myself and our relationship. _____ _____

*Scale:
0-2 sinking in quicksand
3-4 struggling in the jungle
5-6 surviving in the jungle
7-8 thriving in the jungle
9-10 swinging in the treetops

Author Biography

Dr. Terry Parsons is a husband, dad, psychotherapist, university consultant, teacher, minister, and the developer of COMMIT seminars for dating and engaged couples and THRIVE seminars for married couples. He earned his Doctor of Ministry degree in Pastoral Counseling from Southern Methodist University and his Ph.D. in Clinical Psychology from The Fielding Institute. His professional affiliations include: American Association for Marriage and Family Therapy, American Psychological Association, American Group Psychotherapy Association, and American Association of Pastoral Counselors. Dr. Parsons is an avid baseball fan, loves to travel, and genuinely cares about people. His mission through his counseling, speaking, and writing is to help people in a world of troubled marriages and painful divorces to find the right mates, develop intimate relationships, and have thriving, lifetime marriages.

Notes